Destination Wisdom
Discovering the Journey

Adam Rondeau, Ph.D.

Eagle Publications
Shreveport, Louisiana

Destination Wisdom
Discovering the Journey

Copyright © 2020 by Adam Rondeau, Ph.D.

ISBN 13:9781088515242

Scripture quotations are from the Holy Bible King James Version unless otherwise indicated.

Editing and Design: Book Creators for Pastors; Kit R. Olsen, M.A.

Compass image courtesy of Evasplace / Freepik

Published by Eagle Publications
Shreveport, Louisiana

Printed in the United States of America.

I dedicate this work to my wife, Joni. Apart from her encouragement, inspiration, and at times, prodding—this book would never have become a reality. She is also my great helpmeet, as together we endeavor to lead our children (Anna, Curt, Josiah, and Micah) on their journey toward wisdom. Joni embodies the wise woman of Proverbs 31 and every area of my life is better with her. Many women have lived virtuously, but Joni surpasses them all (Proverbs 31:29).

Who can find a virtuous woman?
for her price is far above rubies (Proverbs 31:10).

Contents

Introduction 1

PART ONE
The Destination 5

Chapter One
Know Where You're Going 7

Chapter Two
The Primary Pursuit 13
Defining Wisdom 14

Chapter Three
First Class Travel 17
An Attribute of Divinity 18

Chapter Four
Traveling Companions 21
"An Excellent Spirit" 22
A Person of Understanding 23
"The Key of Knowledge" 24
Void of Understanding 26
The Power of the Key of Knowledge 26
Wisdom, Understanding and Knowledge 27

PART TWO
The Journey 29

Chapter Five
The Boarding Call 31
Wisdom Is Not a Secret 32
God Is Calling for Our Attention 32
Hearing God's Voice 33
Get God's Attention 34

Chapter Six
"This is Your Captain Speaking" 37
The Good Guys 38
The Bad Guys 40
Starting the Journey 40

Chapter Seven
Starting the Journey Off Right 43
Defining: "The Fear of the Lord" 44
Fear Is Contagious 45
Fear That Is Caught—Not Taught 46
The Law of the Home 48

PART THREE
The Roadmap 55

Chapter Eight
The Five Travelers 57

Chapter Nine
A Simple Start 61
The Simple Defined 62
Guiding the Simple 63
God Takes Special Interest in the Simple 65
The Needs of the Simple 68
Preserving the Simple 70
A Turning Point 75

Chapter Ten
Do Not Enter 77
The Scorner 78
The Fool 81

Chapter Eleven
Strategies for Positive Growth 85
Discipline 85
Unfit for Office 88
Fools Refuse to Receive Instruction 88
Hope for the Fool 89

Chapter Twelve
The Final Destination 91
The Prudent 91
Prudence Is NOT the Same As Wisdom 96
The Wise 97

PART FOUR
The Transportation 105

Chapter Thirteen
Purity First 107

A Startling Contrast 109
How Sex in the Culture Affects the Journey 110
Desire Righteousness 111

Chapter Fourteen
"Put a Knife to Thy Throat" 113
An Appetite for Righteousness 115
An Appetite for Wickedness 116
The Lure of Wickedness 117
A Passion for Righteousness 119

Chapter Fifteen
Character Counts 121
Character's Role 123
The Case for Character 124
It Is Your Destiny! 126
Building Character 126
Molded Through Modeling 134
In Conclusion 134

Notes 137

Bibliography 143

Introduction

A MASS EXODUS IS taking place in the Christian church all throughout the United States. Young adults (and even some older lifelong professing believers of Jesus Christ) are leaving in droves "giving heed to seducing spirits and doctrines of devils" (1 Timothy 4:1). This departure is occurring at a rate of nearly 2 out of 3 young people. This widespread abandonment of the faith is both alarming and disturbing. Its ramifications are far-reaching and will have an effect on future generations. I have witnessed this phenomenon firsthand in my twenty-plus years in ministry.

The relativistic impulses of several generations have scorched the morality of our Judea-Christian heritage to the extent that this generation now mirrors the adulterous woman of Proverbs 30:20. These deceived individuals sit at the table of immorality and gorge on sins only to leave the table of their debauchery declaring, "I've done nothing wrong!" And they take their hedonistic revelry one step further, declaring that what they are doing is "right"—calling good evil and evil good! (Isaiah 5:20). The Scriptures tell us that this is not the first time this type of blasphemous insurrection took hold of a nation. The book of Proverbs provides a vivid description of a similar time in ancient Israel:

> "To deliver thee from the way of the evil man, from the man that speaketh froward things; who leave the paths of uprightness, to walk in the ways of darkness; who rejoice to do evil, *and* delight in the frowardness of the wicked; whose ways are crooked, and they froward in their paths: To deliver

thee from the strange woman, even from the stranger which flattereth with her words; which forsaketh the guide of her youth, and forgetteth the covenant of her God" (Proverbs 2:12-17).

People of that day were abandoning God's precepts in favor of wicked self-indulgent behavior. They were forgetting the covenant that God had made with them. They surrendered to immorality and iniquity. In our country today, it is as if history is repeating itself. A large segment of the population in the United States seems to be forsaking God's ways in favor of evil. The book of Judges describes the cycle of apostasy of the Israelites in their on-again-off-again relationship with their covenant God. These dynamics are nothing new. It has happened over and over again throughout history.

Regardless of how many times Israel repeated the cycle, God, would always take her back (when she repented and returned to Him). It is time for our nation to reject the insane foolishness caused by the abandonment of the Judean-Christian heritage of the United States. The Scriptures are clear that wisdom is *needed* to combat this foolishness. Wisdom is available to anyone who will seek it. Gaining wisdom will help prevent the exodus from the faith and repel the spirit of apostasy.

The book of Proverbs is viewed by many as a quaint book of pithy sayings that makes for a good daily devotional due to its convenient number of chapters. Yet buried within the clever sayings and tidbits of wisdom is something much deeper. A careful examination of the overriding message of Proverbs reveals a response to apostasy. Contained within it is the wise man's attempt to combat any type of spiritual defection from occurring within his family.

The book of Proverbs contains a clear message from a father to his son on *how to avoid* the traps of the age and live as a wise man. He implores his son to decidedly reject foolishness in favor of wholeheartedly embracing God's wisdom. The answer to apostasy is living a life totally dedicated to the serious pursuit of wisdom on a daily basis.

This generation does not have to be a statistical anomaly. Our children are not statistics. Just as the wise man of Proverbs demonstrates—it's time to fight for them. It's time to resist the foolish beckoning of the world and instead lead this generation to wisdom. Proverbs is a book exhorting wisdom, elevated to the highest level of importance. It emphasizes wisdom as the *key* to preventing apostasy. It defines and describes wisdom while linking it to Deity, painting vivid imagery through the spiritual analysis of the characterizations of five types of people. The wisdom extolled in Proverbs is built on unwavering solid moral ground.

The message specifically cited in Proverbs 2:1-12 contains within it the cure for stopping defection. Ideally, if wisdom is desired and faithfully pursued, then the exodus from the Church will be prevented and the spirit of apostasy will be shattered:

> "My son, if thou wilt receive my words, and hide my commandments with thee; so that thou incline thine ear unto wisdom, and apply thine heart to understanding; Yea, if thou criest after knowledge and liftest up thy voice for understanding; if thou seekest her as silver, and searchest for her as for hid treasures; then shalt thou understand the fear of the LORD, and find the knowledge of God.

> For the LORD giveth wisdom: out of his mouth cometh knowledge and understanding. He layeth up sound wisdom for the righteous: he is a buckler to them that walk uprightly. He keepeth the paths of judgment, and preserveth the way of his saints. Then shalt thou understand righteousness, and judgment, and equity; yea, every good path.

> When wisdom entereth into thine heart, and knowledge is pleasant unto thy soul; Discretion shall preserve thee, understanding shall keep thee: To deliver thee from the way of the evil man, from the man that speaketh froward things."

The book of Proverbs is a personal passion of mine. I have memorized it in its entirety—read, studied and meditated on it for years. The insight into life and relationships that the book provides is of utmost value. I have written from the framework of a strong belief in the inspiration of the Scriptures and an understanding that salvation is available only through faith alone in Christ Jesus. The wisdom of Proverbs is indeed needed. Parents, pastors and spiritual leaders need to pursue wisdom and lead others to it. The path to wisdom is a journey that spans a lifetime. It remains to this day the journey of my life.

Part One

The Destination

Chapter One

⚓

Know Where You're Going

For whoso findeth me findeth life,
and shall obtain favour of the LORD.
Proverbs 8:35

VACATION! THAT WORD can stir up a lot of emotions and fond memories. I will never forget one vacation I took with my family as a teenager. My father was what we often referred to as a "tentmaker pastor." He pastored a church without receiving a salary. In order to provide for our family he worked another full-time job in addition to fulfilling his pastoral duties. The pastoral ministry was a family mission. We were all very involved and active in the work of the ministry and our lives could get quite hectic. Somehow planning a vacation had fallen through the cracks that year, and we were at a point that particular summer when we just needed to get away for a while—and we did! It was rather spontaneous and we literally just decided one morning to pack up into the van and set out west on the highway.

"Where are we going?" someone asked.

My father replied, "I was thinking we could go to Lake George. I used to go there when I was a kid. It was a lot of fun."

"Did you find a hotel?" my mother asked.

Dad very nonchalantly replied, "Ah, we'll just look around and find something when we get there. Shouldn't be hard. There are all kind of places to stay out there."

This was before booking hotels online was available. There were no cell phones widely available so we would have to rely upon stopping in at hotels one at a time to check pricing and availability. The drive to Lake George was a solid three and a half hours, but we stopped along the way for some site seeing. When we arrived later that afternoon we began to search for some accommodations. To our great surprise, we felt like Joseph and Mary as depicted in the nativity scene. We found again and again that there was "no room at the inn" anywhere in the vicinity. We ate some dinner and started to expand our search but every place we checked had no vacancies.

It was getting late so we started heading back east stopping along the highway checking for hotels with vacancies. I remember falling asleep at some point and being jolted awake by a stop at a hotel. My mother went inside to check if there were any rooms available, but to our disappointment she came out shaking her head indicating that there was no vacancy. Seven tired and cranky people were confined in a family van heading into the wee hours of the early morning; what was supposed to be a relaxing getaway was turning into a nightmare.

We kept heading east toward home and still nothing was available. But finally, we found a place. It was close to two in the morning and although the hotel was only a half hour away from our home, we stayed there until the next day. We learned our lesson and never again went on a vacation without a plan. Nevertheless, our family still had some fun and to this day we rib our dad about that trip. Our problem was that we started off our journey without even knowing our final destination. It's tough to arrive somewhere when you don't know where you're going!

GET WISDOM!

Proverbs 4:7 states, "Wisdom is the principal thing, therefore get wisdom…" There is no such thing as a wisdom lottery with a few random lucky winners. Attaining wisdom is a purposeful journey requiring a serious commitment—a destination to pursue. It is a lifelong process.

For many, wisdom is understood to be simply a right of old age which the elderly have by virtue of their life experiences. Some see it as a natural talent or something that people with good genes are privy to. Some others have a cartoonish superstitious perspective in that God strikes some lucky people with it. They may see the dispensation of wisdom as God sending bolts of lightning with which He is randomly striking individuals. When the meaning of wisdom is misconstrued, then trying to get it becomes like our family vacation without a specific preplanned destination.

Solomon, the principal contributor of the book of Proverbs, was the wisest man to ever live. He was blessed directly by God with a wise and understanding heart. He did not receive a lightning strike impartation. No, not at all. God came to him in a dream and gave Solomon one wish. He used that wish to ask for wisdom. Solomon wasn't struck with wisdom by God like some cosmic lightning bolt. He pursued it.

Wisdom is a lifelong endeavor to attain God's best in life. Being wise is a lifestyle that demonstrates and reflects the principles of God's Word. This principle should be especially successfully exhibited in a Christian's life. A lifestyle is a choice, not some sort of rigid edict that must be carried out. Our culture has pushed the notion that one's lot in life is genetic and something a person must live with. But that is not reality. The reality is that a person *can* change his or her lifestyle status and pursue another. The American dream has shown time and time again that with hard work and persistence, people can "pull themselves up by the bootstraps."

> Wisdom is a lifelong endeavor to attain God's best in life.

The book of Proverbs demonstrates that people can increase their standard of living and move to the highest level of the wise. This understanding is important because it takes away any limitations when seeking wisdom. When wisdom becomes something that can be pursued it removes the threshold of age and diminishes low expectations in every ethnic and socio-economic class. If wisdom is a destination that takes a personal commitment, then anyone can successfully complete the journey.

Wisdom does not only belong to a select elite, it is available to everyone, exactly as God intended. "If any of you lack wisdom, let him ask of God, that giveth to all men liberally, and upbraideth not; and it shall be given him" (James 1:5). Two very important factors play into the pursuit of wisdom. While not co-dependent, they are connected in their relevance: Wisdom requires both *desire* and *leadership*.

DESIRE

"Through desire a man, having separated himself, seeketh and intermeddleth with all wisdom" (Proverbs 18:1). When it comes to taking the journey to wisdom, you "Gotta wanna." It has to be more than fleeting curiosity. When I was twelve years old the great Larry Bird retired from basketball and I wanted to take his place. It was a deep desire I had, and that desire to achieve such a high status drove me to constant practice—so much so that it was rare to see me without a basketball in my hand when I was between the ages 12 to 15.

Around the age of 15, I transitioned to a different pursuit. My desire changed from wanting to be a great basketball player to wanting to be the greatest Christian to walk on the face of the earth since the apostle Paul. I wanted wisdom and God's will for my life.

Solomon also had a deep desire for wisdom. That desire was so ingrained within him that even in his sleep—while dreaming—wisdom was what he asked for when God approached him. It was not a whim. It was a true desire. Desire will drive you to undertake a journey to attain wisdom (or whatever that desire may be). Only when desire is present will an individual separate himself from the pack and "Go for it!" with all he or she has. If you truly don't want something, you won't get it.

LEADERSHIP

Desire for wisdom without leadership isn't enough to get you to your destination. Arriving at a destination requires obtaining the right directions on the right road. Whenever I am driving to a location I've never been to before, there's almost always a voice coming from my GPS (Global Positioning System) telling me what direction to go and when to turn. I need directions to arrive at my destination.

My desire to be the greatest basketball player ever wasn't enough to even get me to a varsity high school team. All the practice in the world wouldn't be enough without proper coaching. In the same way, the desire to obtain wisdom requires good leadership. The Scriptures are to serve as the guiding influence for our lives. They are indeed "the lamp unto our feet and the light into our path" (Psalm 119:105).

While the Scriptures are the ultimate guide, they also describe additional leadership serving in unison along the journey. The book of Proverbs gives very clear relevance to the special role of the kind of leadership necessary for success on the journey to wisdom.

Again and again the messages in the book of Proverbs demonstrate the essential elements of a father giving instruction to his son. It is this instruction that will ultimately lead the son to wisdom. Like the GPS navigating system, leadership is essentially the voice of God-given authority guiding those under the influence of that leadership on the journey toward wisdom.

Parents, pastors, mentors and other godly influences are significant elements of the wisdom leadership team. For this reason, the leadership that one chooses to submit to should be carefully vetted. Take care not only in the leadership which you place yourself under but also the leadership you place your family under. Be sure that your chosen leadership is highly-qualified to direct others toward godly wisdom.

Leadership requires someone to lead and someone to follow. For leadership to occur both must be in action simultaneously. Proverbs is essentially a leadership book. The main plot of the book is that of a father attempting to lead his son toward wisdom. The ongoing message of the leader is to remind the follower that he must hear and receive instruction in order to successfully arrive at his destination.

Instruction means nothing if it is not carefully followed. So many people attending church today are sitting in pews pretending to submit to the leadership of their pastor. In reality, they are completely ignoring his guidance and instruction. Only a genuine desire to gain wisdom can provide the impetus to accept and follow instruction.

The combination of desire and leadership are like twin propellers on the journey to wisdom. When one is missing or dysfunctional—a crash and burn will likely happen. Leaders need to give the instruction that guides others toward wisdom. Desire will create the willingness to receive the instruction. Desire and leadership, together, are what it takes to successfully reach one's destination.

Are you satisfied with where you and your family are regarding wisdom? Are you ready to begin or continue the journey to wisdom? Desire and leadership are what it takes to get there. But do you know where you are going? A proper understanding of wisdom must precede the journey so that you have a journey with a destination.

Points to Ponder

- Do you have misconceptions about what wisdom really is?

- Have you bought into the cultural misnomer that a person is born to live a certain lifestyle and cannot change?

- Do you have the desire to arrive at wisdom and does that desire include willingness to receive instruction?

Chapter Two

✝

The Primary Pursuit

W HEN I WAS fourteen years old my family set out on an adventure somewhat different from our other vacations. We traveled to the other side of the U.S. to Spokane, Washington—where a family member was about to get married. One of my little sisters had an important role in the wedding celebration; my parents had agreed to allow her to be the flower girl. The night before the wedding, the rehearsal was to be held at the chapel followed by a dinner.

The chapel was at a university campus in Spokane, so we headed out to the university and searched for the building where the event was taking place. We drove continuously around the grounds multiple times desperately searching for that one particular building, but could not find it. Finally, my dad stopped and asked someone for directions. It turns out that Spokane has several universities in close proximity. We were not able to find the building because we were on the wrong campus! Once we knew which campus to go to we were able to finally arrive at our destination.

Realizing the need to travel toward wisdom is important, but if we are to truly know where we are going then we must know exactly what defines wisdom. We also need to make sure we are going in the right direction on the right road.

Defining Wisdom

If we are to arrive at our destination then we must be able to define wisdom. With wisdom, as with so many other things, it is sometimes best to first identify what it is not in order to put aside misconceptions. While it is accurate to say that wisdom brings with it a philosophy of life it is not correct to postulate that wisdom is simply a philosophy. Wisdom is expressed in the book of Proverbs, but it would be misleading to relegate it to simple quaint and pithy sayings. It is naïve to speculate that wisdom is simply using "common sense" to make valid and rational choices that lead to positive outcomes.

While wisdom cannot be condensed into a simple philosophical statement or easily and rationally grasped—it can most certainly be defined. Throughout the Scriptures the pursuit and instruction of wisdom always lead to a common end. Wisdom is a lifestyle in which the individual pursues God's best for daily living. Since wisdom is elevated in the Scriptures to be "the principal thing" and should be our primary pursuit, it must therefore not supplant but rather encompass all that God desires for our lives. For instance, wisdom does not replace righteousness, it includes it. Wisdom is not more important than obedience to God; the *pursuit* of wisdom will *always* result in obedience to God.

> As one reads through that material, one quickly recognizes that wisdom was a personal life dynamic that enabled one to assimilate, sort, and categorize the elements and issues of life so as to provide a meaningful synthesis. Its wide span encompasses the struggle of a righteous man to understand his suffering and the limp efforts of a lazy man to overcome his sloth. —Dr. C. Hassell Bullock

Wisdom is a state of being. It is truly living life the way God intended. Often times in the Old Testament many references are made to individuals who had wisdom in certain areas. That wisdom is also often described as given by God. But that type of wisdom can be classified as more of a talent. For example; engraving, sewing, painting, quilting, etc. are talents. The concern here is not with understanding human wisdom or talent, but rather with understanding divine wisdom.

K.S. Kanter describes divine wisdom as "Divine wisdom given by God that enables humans to lead a good and true and satisfying life." The Old Testament concept of divine wisdom must not be abstracted from its practical implications for mankind. Divine wisdom is not only spiritual, it is also practical. It is like having a living faith, not just a concept but also an action. God gives this wisdom priority because He desires for His creation to function in the way He designed and to fulfill the purpose for which He intended.

The New Testament Scriptures present dueling concepts of wisdom. In 1 Corinthians chapters one and two, the stark contrast between worldly wisdom and godly wisdom is described. The "wisdom" of this world must be rejected and opposed. The clash between godly wisdom and worldly wisdom is demonstrated by a viewpoint relative to one's interpretation of any given premise or situation.

While on an overseas mission trip in Asia, I was astounded to find that fried and candied insects are considered quite a delicacy. Apparently, Asians consider fried scorpions an acceptable snack and sell them in shops on the side of the road. My mind, however, could only conceive of stepping on and squashing a scorpion. The idea of chewing on one was completely alien to me. I saw it from a completely different perspective. Creation versus evolution is a debate that is a classic example of two opposing viewpoints. An evolutionist and a creationist can examine the same exact fossil and yet come away with completely different conclusions. This is possible because their assumptions are polar opposites.

> Worldly wisdom is a total antithesis to the things of God.

Worldly wisdom is a total antithesis to the things of God. Worldly wisdom sees through the short-sighted lens of humanism, falsely relegating godly wisdom to foolishness (1 Corinthians 1:18). Those with "worldly" wisdom cannot understand why the Christian can hold to "outdated and old-fashioned" morality. Conversely, Christians are continually appalled by the moral decadence and debauchery embraced by the secular culture. These two opposing worldviews cannot be understood from one another's starting point—because one has its source in God and the other in mankind.

Because true wisdom has its source in God it requires faith. It is only through faith that we can approach God and please Him (Hebrews 11:6). In order to obtain this wisdom we must go to God in faith—it will not be found in the world. It comes directly from above. This is why, according to 1 Corinthians 2:5 we read, "That your faith should not stand in the wisdom of man, but in the power of God."

Even though godly wisdom seems like foolishness to the world, the believer must override any leanings toward humanism. We are seeing record high numbers of people abandoning the faith; they are rejecting godly wisdom in favor of humanism. These short-sighted individuals don't want their worldview to be at odds with the secular world, so they make excuses for violating God's directives. (Christian leaders must guard against these dynamics which can seep into their churches and ministries.)

> "For the time will come when they will not endure sound doctrine; but after their own lusts shall they heap to themselves teachers, having itching ears; and they shall turn away their ears from the truth, and shall be turned unto fables" (2 Timothy 4:3).

Whether in regard to sexuality and marriage, the sanctity of human life or a host of other issues, those who compromise biblical values are trying to integrate humanism with godly wisdom. These differences are truly irreconcilable.

> "There is a way which seemeth right unto a man, but the end thereof are the ways of death" (Proverbs 14:12).

This conflict is not merely a culture war. It extends deeper than the culture and into the spiritual realm. This is the generational spiritual warfare in which the soldiers of Christ must be engaged. The pursuit of godly wisdom is so vital. Its span fully extends into all areas of life providing stability and direction.

Points to Ponder

- Are you able to state a concise definition of wisdom?

- Have you noticed or experienced the vast and distinctive difference between worldly and godly wisdom?

Chapter Three

⚓

First Class Travel

I PARTICIPATED IN MY first significant international trip when I traveled to Thailand in late 2016. The longest leg of the journey was from New York to China. The plane flew directly north over the Arctic Circle transitioning to a southern trajectory as we crossed Siberia into China. I never had the chance to look out the window because I was seated directly in the middle of the plane; I was blessed with an aisle seat and an empty seat to my right.

My return flight, though, was very different. While waiting to board the plane there was an elderly gentleman in line with a horrible persistent cough—the kind of a cough that makes you worry about communicable diseases. In addition to that, he apparently had never been instructed in proper coughing protocol because he never once covered his mouth. At the end of every coughing spasm he would make a strange throat-clearing sound that made his cough sound wet and even more contagious. He was receiving many disdainful looks from several of the other passengers, but it didn't seem to faze him. I should have prayed for him while waiting there in that long line. Instead, I thought to myself, *I feel bad for the poor sap that has to sit next to that guy.*

Finally, I made it to my seat. This time I was in the middle seat with someone on either side of me. There was a sweet young lady in the window seat to my left, but no one on my right when I sat down—so I was optimistic that perhaps I would strike gold again and have an empty seat next to me. This was not to be, however, as I soon discovered that I was the poor sap that would sit next to the elderly coughing gentleman for the next twelve hours. It was a long twelve hours! There were hundreds of people on the flight and it seemed that we were all crammed in like sardines in a can. And I felt like the sardine in the middle of the bottom row of the can.

After landing, and during the disembarking process I began to feel a twinge of envy as I walked past the first-class cabin of the plane. For twelve hours I had been seated in a small center aisle next to the poster person for Robitussin. The first-class passengers had their own private suites. They had chairs that could lay back into a couch, a small desk with drawers to hold personal items and there was a dividing wall or an entire aisle separating them from anyone else. I remember thinking, *That would have been nice!*

I have flown to many locations around the U.S.A. and a few around the world, but have never enjoyed the luxury of flying first class. My wife, however, has been bumped up to first class on multiple occasions. (She tells me it's great!) The central idea of first class travel is that you have it better than the rest of the passengers. On this journey—wisdom is located in the first-class cabin.

An Attribute of Divinity

Proverbs chapter eight delivers a very vivid description of godly wisdom. The description given actually associates wisdom with many other divine attributes. Verses 6 through 9 demonstrate how wisdom is perfection and a source of righteousness. The Scriptures are clear that the Source of righteousness and the only perfect Person is Christ Jesus. It goes on

> Since wisdom's source is God Himself, its pursuit equates to a pursuit of God.

further to claim in verses 15 through 16 that wisdom bequeaths power to those who are in authority. The Scriptures are consistent in their message that all authority stems from God and God alone.

Verses 22 through 31 in chapter eight go on to suggest that wisdom exists in eternity beyond the scope of physical time in that it existed before the creation of the universe. It further contends that wisdom had at least an observational role in the very Creation itself by its presence in the establishment of the air, sea and land during those first six days. This observatory role changed to one of interaction with mankind upon the completion of God's creation that continues to presently exist.

Many have speculated that the depiction of wisdom in those verses is actually a description of Christ. While there are many divine connections to this portrayal of wisdom, a full exegesis of the verses rules out that they are a description of Christ. The feminine attribution and the passiveness of the role she plays in Creation should lead us to conclude that this is a poetic description of wisdom as a divine attribute.

The entirety of Proverbs chapter eight is a vivid personification of a lady named Wisdom. Lady Wisdom is poetically described in terms that express her as a divine attribute. Clearly, Lady Wisdom is a companion of God Himself. Through the use of poetry and personification, the Scriptures paint a picture that clearly depict Wisdom's Source as God Almighty. This is why wisdom is "the principal thing."

A pursuit of wisdom equates to a pursuit of God. You cannot separate true wisdom from God. That is also why wisdom is accessible and available to everyone. The God who provides salvation to everyone through His Son is the same God who will liberally distribute wisdom to those who seek it (James 1:5). After we understand what wisdom is and have a working definition of it, it is essential to connect it to its Source—God Himself. Wisdom's priority and prominence only make sense when it is connected to its Divine Root. Why even go on the journey unless the destination's promises are worth it? Since wisdom stems from God, the journey's promises are precious and solid.

The famous conquistador, Juan Ponce de Leon, searched for the fountain of life in Florida long before it became the retirement center that it is today. It was an elusive search that failed. The fountain of true wisdom springs forth from God Almighty and will lead one to success if carefully navigated. It is worth the effort. On this journey, wisdom is in the first class cabin with God and that is where we should aspire to be.

POINTS TO PONDER

- The Source of wisdom is God alone.
- Am I looking in the right place for it?
- Do I consider wisdom a worthy pursuit?

Chapter Four

⚓

Traveling Companions

Through wisdom is an house builded;
and by understanding it is established:
And by knowledge shall the chambers
be filled with all precious and pleasant riches.
Proverbs 24:3-4

M Y MIND WAS reeling as I was rushing up the stairs. "You're gonna blow it now," I told myself as I reached into my pants pocket for my dorm room keys. I hurriedly unlocked the door and rushed into my room and quickly began to change my clothes. I was in my final year at Bible college and had recently been appointed as the youth pastor of a small country church which I attended. I only had about a half hour before I needed to be at church for the youth service. I was completely clueless as to what I was going to use for the teaching that night. It wasn't that I had been ignoring my devotions or neglecting the Scriptures, I was just bone dry. I didn't have anything new to talk about. Sure, I could have recycled some message or teaching in my files but I wanted to give those kids something special. I wanted something fresh off the altar, but I had nothing.

"Just take a deep breath and pray," I told myself. I knew God was faithful and if I opened my mouth he would fill it (Psalm 81:10). So I grabbed my Bible and knelt beside my bed. As I did that, a note I had stuffed inside my Bible cover fell out. I bent down to pick it up and saw that it was from my aunt. I had read it before, but I wasn't sensing anything else was coming so I opened it up and read it again. My aunt had written a simple note of encouragement to me that included all the sweet things that an aunt would say to her nephew. (I could almost feel her pinch my cheeks through that note!) At the end, she added this statement, "You have always been an excellent young man (Daniel 6:3)."

Although I had read the note before, my aunt's message seemed to resonate with me when I needed it the most. I took the cue and opened my Bible and found that Daniel had "an excellent spirit." Then the wheels of my mind began to turn! *How does one get an excellent* spirit? I quickly grabbed my concordance and began to search through the Scriptures. In that short thirty minutes, the Holy Spirit gave me a message for the youth group that night. It didn't matter to me that only three youth showed up. I had fresh bread of life to serve that night (John 6:35). It was during that brief Bible study forced by necessity that I first began to come to the realization that wisdom does not travel alone. Wisdom has two very important traveling companions we need to get to know: understanding and knowledge.

"AN EXCELLENT SPIRIT"
The devil is looking for unsuspecting talented young people to manipulate for his distorted purposes (1 Peter 5:8). He tries to go after the best and the brightest in the Church and hits them with his entire arsenal. This was certainly the case during the time of Daniel. The entire reason that Daniel was even in Babylon was due to a wicked king looking for new talent to further his purposes.

> "And the king spake unto Ashpenaz the master of his eunuchs, that he should bring certain of the children of Israel, and of the king's seed, and of the princes; children in whom was no blemish, but well favoured, and skilful in all wisdom, and cunning in knowledge, and understanding science, and such as had ability in them to stand in the king's palace, and whom they might teach the learning and the tongue of the Chaldeans" (Daniel 1:3-4).

Daniel's training in Babylon was taking place in an environment that was very much comparable to the college environment pervasive throughout American academia today. He was in a place where his mind was being fed all kinds of philosophies and doctrines that were the polar opposite of what he had learned in his homeland of Israel. Those teachings were antithetical to the Holy Scriptures from which he had received instruction. Yet in the midst of such a society, Daniel became a bright and shining light. He was recognized as having an "excellent spirit." This set Daniel apart from others.

What was it that gave Daniel this excellent spirit? It was not Daniel's higher than average intelligence or his advanced education. It was not an understanding of mathematics, physics, economics or any other academic pursuit. What set him apart was an understanding brought about by a knowledge of the holy things of God and His Word.

When an individual can assimilate the Word of God into a comprehensive awareness of just how God intends that life to be lived, he has the understanding that brings about excellence. Daniel had understanding because he was acutely aware of, and could recognize God's plans and designs. He knew what God wanted, thus he had understanding. This understanding does not require special diplomas or degrees. It is available to the illiterate tribesman in the deepest darkest jungles just as it is available to the highly educated in the halls of academia. It is an understanding that requires a knowledge of God and His Word.

A PERSON OF UNDERSTANDING
"He that hath knowledge spareth his words: and a man of understanding is of an excellent spirit" (Proverbs 17:27). I can vividly remember as a young boy around the age of five, being very confused by Psalm 23. My parents were regularly reading it to me, my brother and sister for evening devotions. The last verse always left me perplexed. (My father would often finish the psalm by singing the last verse.)

We would also sing the words from Psalm 23 in church. As we sang the song I would wonder about the meaning of the words. My five-year-old mind thought it had "goodness" and "mercy" figured out, but because my young mind was confusing the word "surely" with the name Shirley, I would always wonder, *Who in the world is this Shirley girl and why is she following me?*

One night I mustered the courage and questioned my father. "Dad, who is Shirley? You know, the lady who is following us?" He reared his head back and started to laugh. I didn't have any understanding of what the verse was saying. Of course, he explained it to me and I was finally able to come to a point of comprehending what the verse really meant.

This kind of confusion in young minds is certainly common. My wife had a similar understanding of the word when she was very young. She always thought it was cool that her grandmother, Shirley, had her name in the Bible until she came to realize that isn't actually the case.

While singing "America the Beautiful" during a church service my young daughter suddenly became enlightened. For so many years she had misunderstood the lyrics. She turned to me as we were singing the song and said, "Oh it's not Robin Hood! It's brotherhood. Now I get it!" I had to pinch myself that time to keep from laughing out loud. Understanding words and their meanings is an important element in the development of young lives.

"The Key of Knowledge"

"Woe unto you, lawyers! For ye have taken away the key of knowledge: ye entered not in yourselves, and them that were entering in ye hindered" (Luke 11:52). When I was a young teenager just beginning high school my younger sister was in elementary school starting to learn the concept of borrowing and subtracting. She was really struggling with it and asked me to help her.

Others had tried to explain it to her but she simply wasn't getting it. So I decided to give it a go. Instead of doing the technical description I decided to explain it by assigning the digits to a persona of the Three Stooges. It started out that Moe didn't have enough to subtract from. So he went over to Larry and asked to borrow. Since Larry was a zero and had nothing to give, Moe knocked him down and took one from Curly who was next door to Larry.

I have no idea why it worked, but my sister completely related to the Three Stooges and her understanding of math started to click. She would be doing math problems and I could hear her muttering the names of the Three Stooges. It was silly, but Moe, Larry and Curly were a key to her understanding math concepts. When it comes to the things of God that lead to wisdom, knowledge is the key that leads to understanding.

Understanding comes through a knowledge of God's Word. Without this knowledge there will be no understanding and wisdom will be a foreign concept. Knowledge is the key, but that key is all too often neglected. The United States of America is becoming biblically illiterate at an accelerated pace. The reason for this is that so few Americans have a desire to actually read the Bible.

The Barna Group reported in 2016 that only about one-third of all American adults read the Bible at least once a week. The millennial generation bottoms out that trend with only 24 percent. God has given His people a divine revelation in the Scriptures and yet the majority of Americans are ignoring it.

The prophet Hosea spoke of the destructive effects that a lack of knowledge of the Holy Scriptures can cause. God rejects this form of ignorance as inexcusable, and ultimately it is the following generation that will pay the price for the previous generation's neglect.

> "My people are destroyed for lack of knowledge: because thou hast rejected knowledge, I will also reject thee, that thou shalt be no priest to me: seeing thou hast forgotten the law of thy God, I will also forget thy children" (Hosea 4:6).

Not only is the key of knowledge being ignored, but it is also being forcibly taken away. This struggle is most precisely exemplified by two Supreme Court decisions made in 1962 and 1963.

In 1962 the Court decided in Engel v. Vitale that prayer in the public schools was unconstitutional. It followed that decision with yet another, the next year in Abington School District v. Schempp when it ruled that Bible reading in public schools was also illegal.

With those two decisions the Supreme Court, a body of nine unelected and unaccountable individuals, forcibly took away the key of knowledge from the majority of American youth. Ever since then public schools have been on a path of destruction. Truly there is the famine of hearing the words of the Lord of which the prophet Amos spoke (Amos 8:11).

Yet so much of this is paradoxical as there has never been a time in history when the Word of God was so readily available. The American Bible Society reports that a whopping 87 percent of households possess a Bible. Not just one, but the average is three per household. Bookstores are full of devotionals and study tools—not to mention the instantaneous access to seemingly limitless teachings available on the Internet, and 24/7 from Christian radio and television broadcasting stations.

Void of Understanding

Christ harshly rebuked the lawyers of his day for making the Law so complex and distorted that no one could understand it. His harsh words in Luke 11:52 also apply to life today, "Woe unto you, lawyers! For ye have taken away the key of knowledge: ye entered not in yourselves, and them that were entering in ye hindered." There are many factors at play in our society that have done this same thing. Whether through legislation or perpetual undermining of the inspiration of the Scriptures, the key of knowledge is under attack.

Taking the key of knowledge away has resulted in a generation that is "void of understanding" just as the young man described in Proverbs chapter seven. Because society as a whole lacks knowledge and understanding of the holy precepts of God, they are void of understanding and all moral discernment has been lost. The result is a fragmented society completely unaware of God's purposes and designs for life—which include biblical gender identity, marriage, etc.

America is reeling from generations of youth that have had the key of knowledge withheld from them. The biblical illiteracy and conscious rejection of God's ways in favor of evil divisiveness are a direct result of a void in understanding. Lady Folly has easy access to our youth and she is taking full advantage of leading them astray. It's time to reverse that trend.

The Power of the Key of Knowledge

In 1962 when the Supreme Court first issued its ban on prayer in schools many people in our country were outraged. President John F. Kennedy was in office. He was confronted at a White House news conference about what he thought of the ruling and what could be done. He first contended that it was important to support Supreme Court decisions even when we do not agree with them, but went on to add this sentiment:

> In addition, we have in this case a very easy remedy and that is to pray ourselves. And I would think that it would be a welcome reminder to every American family that we can pray a good deal more at home, we can attend our churches with a good deal more fidelity, and we can make the true meaning of prayer much more important in the lives of all of our children. That power is very much open to us. And I would hope that as a result of this decision that all American parents will intensify their efforts at home.

Oh, that individuals and families would realize that the power of the key of knowledge is very much open to us! It is this knowledge of the holy precepts of God that will bring understanding and an excellent spirit. This type of knowledge is not something that is recognized with a certificate of achievement acknowledging completion of all necessary studies. The knowledge of holiness is a lifelong pursuit which never ends. Also, this knowledge is not simply academic, but also experiential.

In Psalm 73 Asaph describes a time in his life when he was questioning God, and the way things were being done. He was perplexed by what he saw. But when he went into "the sanctuary of God, then he understood their end" (v. 17). It was his experience in the presence of God that illuminated Asaph's knowledge into understanding.

It is so important that the key of knowledge be given and not withheld. The Greek term for knowledge is *gnosis,* meaning "a knowledge gained by experience." Experiencing the presence and power of God through exposure to His Word is what will connect the dots to understanding. This is from where wisdom springs forth.

Wisdom, Understanding and Knowledge

Wisdom begins to express itself in a person's life when an understanding of God and the enormity of who and what He is—is realized. The knowledge of the Creator's holiness is what gives a person an "excellent spirit" (Daniel 6:3). The knowledge of God and his holy attributes bring about an understanding of His plans and purposes. But it is not until that knowledge and understanding are applied to a person's life that wisdom is born. "Wisdom is before him that hath understanding" (Proverbs 17:24a).

Points to Ponder

- Do I have an understanding of God's purposes and designs for life?
- Am I applying the key of knowledge to my own life through reading, studying, meditation, and application of Scriptures?
- Am I successful in communicating my understanding of the knowledge of God's holiness to others around me, in particular my family?

Part Two

The Journey

Chapter Five

⚓

The Boarding Call

Doth not wisdom cry?
Proverbs 8:1

DURING ONE OF my travels by air I had an extended layover. To pass the time I found a quiet corner and took out my laptop and kept myself busy with some work. As a concentration aid, I put on my headphones and listened to music to drown out the background noise. I noticed movement for the initial call for seating but decided I would wait and take my time. I wasn't in a hurry to be seated on the plane and decided to let the other passengers board ahead of me.

After a considerable amount of time I looked up from my work and took off my headphones. I heard something I had never heard before when traveling; I heard my name being called out over the public address system of the airport instructing me to report to the gate for boarding and departure. I had been so engrossed in what I was doing and distracted by the music in my ears that I missed all of the boarding calls and almost missed my flight. If I had missed my flight it would not have been for a lack of effort by the airline personnel to make me aware of the boarding process. It would simply have been because I either didn't hear or purposely ignored the calls.

Wisdom is making a public cry for boarding! A few are hearing and heeding the call. And sadly, many are missing or ignoring the call.

WISDOM IS NOT A SECRET

Wisdom is not a hidden secret. It is quite the opposite. Proverbs chapter 8 describes Lady Wisdom as a very vocal advocate for herself. She is pictured as standing on high places where she is easily visible—at intersections of roads giving access to the multitudes who travel those pathways. She is at the city gates where everyone must pass through to enter the city.

It is from these strategic locations that Lady Wisdom calls out to all who will hear, to come and partake of what she has to offer. She offers her blessings to all those who will hear her call and heed her warnings. "She standeth in the top of high places, by the way in the places of the paths. She crieth at the gates, at the entry of the city, at the coming in at the doors. Unto you, O men, I call; and my voice is to the sons of man" (Proverbs 8:2-4).

> It has been established that the Source of wisdom is God Himself.

A very important connection must be made at this point. It has been established that the Source of wisdom is God Himself. Therefore, the connection to the voice of wisdom and the voice of God must be made. The picture of Lady Wisdom calling out should also create an imagery of the voice of God. Indeed, the call of wisdom is the voice of God.

GOD IS CALLING FOR OUR ATTENTION

The lengths to which God will go to get the attention of people is fascinating. Moses had an encounter with a burning bush to draw him out of his seclusion in the desert. The almost comical occurrence of a talking donkey used to get Balaam's attention exemplifies the lengths to which God will go to get the attention of those He wants to reach. God is interested in gaining the attention of His creation. The fervent and diligent cry of wisdom in Proverbs chapter 8 is a reflection of God trying to call His people away from foolishness and into His ways of wisdom.

The problem, however, is that humanity is often so distracted by everything else in this world that there is a propensity to totally miss the call of Almighty God. So often people miss what is directly in front of them and ignore nearby voices. I can't tell you the number of times my wife has called out to me from only a few feet away, but I did not hear her. I was too distracted by other things, and not paying attention.

Then there is the scenario of teenagers whose parents are yelling at them for the *fifth time* to go and take out the trash. But the teens are so distracted and/or inattentive during the first four attempts at gaining their attention, that the parents get very frustrated. Yet the teens genuinely never heard the call of their parents. This is not to excuse them, it is meant to explain a common tendency.

Most of us are a distracted people with very few moments of quiet. Various types of media constantly flash before our eyes and flood our ears. Recent studies point to the increased use of media screens as an explanation for the drop in average attention spans from twelve seconds to eight seconds (over a fifteen year period). It was found that even the goldfish beat us with an attention span of nine seconds! Obviously, people have the capacity for a much longer attention span. But there are so many distractions vying for our attention for which the of cry of wisdom must compete.

Even though wisdom is obviously making her plea the call can be missed. An example of this would be when a teenager is texting while walking, and walks into a pole in front of him. The mishap doesn't even phase him. He just sidesteps a little and keeps going never looking up from his phone. He is in a state of distraction and nothing else can get his attention. In order to even start on the journey to wisdom the boarding call must be heard. The call is going out but too few are paying attention.

Chapter three in the book of Revelation describes the church of Laodecia. That church was so distracted by their consumption of the things of this world that they missed God when He wanted to get their attention. Jesus was standing at their door and knocking, just waiting for someone to let Him in. He said, "If any man hear my voice, and open the door…" (Revelation 3:20). God was desperately trying to get their attention, but they were not listening. The voice of wisdom is calling to everyone and anyone who will hear. Will you pay attention?

HEARING GOD'S VOICE

In 1 Samuel chapter three, God was trying to speak to and get the attention of the young boy, Samuel, while he lay asleep one night. He called out to Samuel with an audible voice. Unfortunately, Samuel didn't recognize God's voice and he was confused by it. He thought it was the voice of the high priest Eli. Three times God called out to Samuel and three times he ran to Eli. Finally, Eli recognized what was happening and taught Samuel how to recognize the voice of God.

The fact is that God is calling to us, yet so few know how to recognize His voice. Giving Him attention is the first step, but the importance of recognition is vital. This is where leadership plays a significant role. Just as Eli helped Samuel to recognize the voice of God, so must modern leadership rise to the challenge of aiding others with that same recognition. If Samuel couldn't recognize God's voice on his own, how many others have missed the voice of God calling to them? This usually happens because those who are in leadership roles fail to guide people who rely on them. The prophet Isaiah said, "And thine ears shall hear a word behind thee, saying, 'This is the way, walk ye in it, when ye turn to the right hand, and when ye turn to the left'" (Isaiah 30:21).

How many people are going the wrong way because they can't identify the voice of God and have no one to help them? Leaders must fulfill their roles in this area. When an individual is willing to receive instruction from authority, he or she will be better equipped to hear wisdom's call. The journey to wisdom requires not only an initial hearing of the call of wisdom, but continual attention to that voice. Wisdom does not just call to receive attention, but to further provide instruction for life, which comes about through familiarity with God's voice.

Abraham was very aware of God's voice. He heard God's initial command to sacrifice Isaac on Mt. Moriah and obeyed. He was also so experienced with the voice of God that he caught the command to stop the sacrifice. I'm sure Isaac was very grateful that his father could clearly discern the voice of God. Wisdom requires such instant recognition of God's voice. Having experience with wisdom's cry plays an important role throughout the journey.

Get God's Attention

My very patient wife and daughter both know how hard it can be to get the attention of the male members of our family at the dinner table. We tend to take dinner very seriously focusing intently on what is before us on our plates. If my wife or daughter need something passed to them they won't just ask for the item—they will specifically call out the name of the person closest to the item in order to get his attention, then ask for the item to be passed. Sadly, we are not always as attentive as we should be.

The same is true so often with wisdom's cry. It goes unheard and unheeded so often because too many individuals are inattentive and miss the voice of God. In Isaiah chapter six, the prophet Isaiah demonstrates tremendous attention to the voice of God. The same year that King Uzziah died, Isaiah saw the Lord in a vision. This demonstrates his faithfulness that even in tribulation he could still see God at work. In this glorious vision of the Lord seated upon His throne in great glory Isaiah heard the Lord speak, "Whom shall I send, and who will go for us?"

Notice that when God spoke from the burning bush He said, "Moses, Moses!" calling a specific person with a specific task. In the middle of the night God spoke into a bed chamber, "Samuel, Samuel!" calling to a specific person with a particular message. That was not the case in Isaiah chapter six. The Lord was making a generic statement that was addressed to no one in particular. God was looking for someone to do something. Even though it was not specifically directed to Isaiah, he heard the call. Isaiah's response was immediate as he replied, "Here am I; send me."

Could it be that Isaiah responded to the Lord in the same way that the little kids in my children's church reply whenever I ask for a volunteer? All I need to do is make the statement that I need a volunteer and immediately little hands will go straight up. Some of them are so anxious to be chosen that they will stand up and start waving their hands while trying to extend them even higher with the other hand. They will start making little monkey-like noises and cry out, "Pick me! Pick me!" This response stands in stark contrast to the typical response of teens. If I ask them a question they will first look around at everyone else to see if any other hands are up. If it looks like it's cool to raise their hands and answer, they will raise their hands to about shoulder's height at an angle that only the teacher can see.

I don't think Isaiah responded like the latter. It is very possible when Isaiah heard that God was calling for someone, that he jumped up with great enthusiasm, waved his arms and cried out, "Here am I; send me." He must have been very enthusiastic because he quickly volunteered upon hearing God's call (even though he had no idea what God wanted). It was a wide-open question that God posed in search of a willing servant, and Isaiah jumped at the chance when he heard the call. God had Isaiah's attention and soon after, it was Isaiah's turn to get God's attention. He gave his attention to God and then tried to get some attention from God. This is the model for responding to wisdom's call.

Wisdom is calling out from the high places and throughout various areas of our lives. The cry is meant for all who will hear and respond. It is an open invitation. When the call of wisdom has the attention of our sons or daughters, they can then begin to pursue it. In order to hear the cry of wisdom we have to *want* to hear it. We have to listen for it. If we listen carefully, we will hear it. The cry of wisdom yearns for a response. Do you hear the call?

Points to Ponder

- Does God have my attention?
- Am I so distracted by the things of this world that I am missing the cry of wisdom?
- How familiar am I with the voice of wisdom (the voice of God)?
- What has been my response to the call of wisdom?

Chapter Six

⚓

"This is Your Captain Speaking"

*Hear counsel, and receive instruction, that thou
mayest be wise in thy latter end.
Proverbs 19:20*

ANYONE WHO HAS ever traveled to a particular destination on a major airline has most assuredly encountered the initial pre-flight instructions given by the flight crew (just before the flight begins). It is typically a prepared statement (probably written by a team of lawyers) presented by a flight attendant. The instructions are intended to inform passengers about safety features and the basic procedures of the flight. The information given is usually very dry and boring. As a frequent flyer I have often found them easy to ignore. I have found one airline to be an exception and seems to encourage their flight attendants to use humor in their presentations.

On one particular flight I had a seat in the first row. The flight attendant presented all the instructions to the passengers through a variety of professional sounding Looney Tune cartoon character voices. I certainly didn't "check out" during that presentation. One of the passengers sitting next to me even recorded the entire presentation and shared it on social media. It has had over five million views. It is without a doubt the most memorable set of flight instructions I have ever received. It was great fun to hear that innovative presentation.

The crew's instructions are often followed by a brief statement from the captain which typically begins with the phrase, "This is your captain speaking…" The captain and the flight attendants are tasked with the responsibility of safely transporting the passengers through the air over hundreds and even thousands of miles at a time.

On the journey to wisdom there are some important key players (tour guides) who are tasked with guiding people toward or away from wisdom. Two types of influences come in contact with the traveler. One is a positive influence leading the individual, assisting in recognizing and following wisdom's cry. The other is a negative influence that distracts from wisdom and leads a person astray. The role of both "tour guides" must be discerned if the journey is to be successful.

The Good Guys

When it comes to the importance of leadership, the key leaders are parents and authority figures. The role that these leaders play is addressed in detail in the following chapters, but I will give a brief overview of their importance in this chapter. Parents and authority figures (i.e., pastors, teachers, and other mentoring influences) have the sacred responsibility of providing leadership and guidance throughout the journey to wisdom. The book of Proverbs places particular emphasis on the leadership role of parents.

Perhaps the most important role that leadership plays is to teach children *how* to recognize the cry of wisdom. An example of this was given in the previous chapter when Eli helped Samuel discern the voice of God. It is important to understand that without the leadership of Eli (as flawed as he was), Samuel would not have been able to recognize God's voice. Eli's leadership in Samuel's life taught him how to recognize the voice of God. The voice of the Lord was precious in that it was rare for anyone to hear from Him—due to the poor spiritual condition of the Israelites. Yet even in those times, Eli acknowledged that God would speak and he could discern His voice. Because of Eli's leadership, Samuel's life and ministry continued to be marked by his familiarity with, and ability to recognize the voice of God.

In addition to teaching Samuel *how* to recognize the voice of God, Eli also taught him how to *respond* to the call of God. Recognition is only the first step, and a proper response is very necessary. Leadership proved invaluable as

Eli went a step further instructing Samuel on *how* to properly respond when he heard God's voice. Proper leadership is essential. How many people have missed the cry of wisdom and passed right by it because they could not recognize and/or were unsure as to how to respond? Parents and authority figures are tasked with the sacred responsibility of leading and guiding in this area.

During the summer of 2017 an 11-year-old boy, Frank Giaccio, was given the privilege of mowing the lawn at the White House. He had written a letter to the President of the United States volunteering for the task. His initiative was rewarded one sunny day. While he was busily mowing the lawn none other than the President of the United States, Donald Trump, came out to speak with him and tell him what a great job he was doing. However, the boy paid him no mind and continued his mowing pattern across the lawn.

> The book of Proverbs places particular emphasis on the leadership role of parents.

President Trump followed him and continued to call out to him, but he just kept on mowing. Finally, a maintenance worker and the boy's father approached him and pointed out that the president was trying to get his attention. He finally stopped for a few seconds and acknowledged the president, but then started mowing again. The president followed him again and was trying to talk to him over the noise of the mower. Finally, the boy's father signed for him to turn the mower off and listen to what the president had to say.

Without the leadership of the boy's father helping him to both acknowledge and appropriately respond to President Trump, the boy might have missed a life-changing opportunity to speak with the President of the United States. This is the vital role that leadership must play in the life of those journeying toward wisdom.

When there is a deficiency in leadership the cry of wisdom will be missed and not responded to appropriately. "Hear counsel, and receive instruction, that thou mayest be wise in thy latter end" (Proverbs 19:20). In addition to guidance, leadership also offers encouragement and motivation for a person's journey toward wisdom. A significant part of leadership stems from personal application of what is trying to be imparted.

In the book of Proverbs the son is encouraged to hear and heed the words of his father. The father's knowledge and life experiences are passed on to the son. The leadership administered by the father serves as an example of inspiration on the journey to wisdom. The role of effective leadership is very much needed but sadly, so many completely miss their destination due to its absence.

THE BAD GUYS

In the book of Proverbs we can see standing in stark contrast to the necessary leadership of parents and authority, the derailing "leadership" and influence of the wicked. The wicked are loathsome and sinful. But their influence *can* be quickly negated. Immediately after the introductory statements of Proverbs in chapter 1:1-7 where wisdom is described, a clear warning is followed regarding the influence of the wicked and the necessity of avoiding their influence (verses 8-19).

The wicked are those who have rejected wisdom and embraced foolishness. They desire to do wrong and follow through with their ungodly actions. The wicked are often presented as peers attempting to exert influence over the lives of our youth. The goal of the wicked is to serve as a distraction on the journey to wisdom. They say, "Come with us," which is to imply that they want to supplant the positive influence of parents and authority. They always seem to be going in the opposite direction away from good leadership.

The method of the wicked is to tempt people with the pleasures of this world. They tantalize with the promise of worldly gain (Proverbs 1:13). This includes the enticement of immoral women who come clothed in the sensual attire of a harlot—pledging pleasures void of any consequence. Yet soon her victims discover that her assurances were empty lies that lead to the way of hell (Proverbs chapter seven).

The wicked are to be avoided and resisted on the journey to wisdom. Their function is to serve as a negative example to the traveler. Those with a wicked agenda should be perceived as warning signs of impending danger that can cause derailment away from the highway of wisdom.

STARTING THE JOURNEY

A very real struggle exists in the realm of leadership. It is often difficult for authority to retain relevance. Just like the dry presentations of so many of the flight attendants that are easily tuned out, the instruction of leadership is often ignored. As a result, many miss the call of wisdom.

Sadly, good leadership is often replaced by the negative influence of the wicked which come cleverly disguised in high-tech formats. It is nearly impossible to compete with animation, movies and video games. Creativity in capturing the attention of those under the authority of good leadership is very necessary. It is very often the greatest challenge to devoted leaders.

A successful journey requires proper leadership that is carefully followed. It is so important to hear the call of wisdom! Once the call of wisdom is recognized and an appropriate response is made, it is time to start the journey.

Points to Ponder

- Can I recognize the call of wisdom and can I lead others to recognize it?

- Do I respond appropriately upon recognizing the call of wisdom and can I also lead others to respond appropriately?

- Take a minute and specifically identify those in your life who can lead you in your journey to wisdom. Thank God for them and acknowledge their influence by submitting to their leadership.

- Identify the people in your life to whom you have the sacred responsibility of leading on their journey to wisdom. Conduct a self-examination of your strategy for leading them. If you can't identify a strategy pray about it and allow the Lord to help you formulate one as you read through the remaining chapters of this book.

Chapter Seven

⚓

Starting the Journey Off Right

The fear of the LORD is the beginning of wisdom:
and the knowledge of the holy is understanding.
Proverbs 9:10

WHILE GROWING UP, my parents took our family on vacations in Maine. It always seemed that no matter how far away the location—the local residents would always say, "Oh, it's about twenty minutes from here." We often found it was actually closer to an hour. Mainers have been stereotyped in comedy sketches and pop-culture for the way they say, "You can't get there from here." The phrase in itself is a bit of a paradox, but it is meant to imply that you need to backtrack and get to a different starting point. When it comes to where many try to start their journey toward wisdom we could say, "You can't get there from here." The Scriptures are clear that a pursuit of wisdom must begin with "the fear of the Lord" (Proverbs 9:10). And as the words of the well-known classic song "Do-Re-Mi" declare, "Let's start at the very beginning. A very good place to start."

DEFINING: "THE FEAR OF THE LORD"

We need to have a healthy fear of the Lord. The phrase "fear of the Lord" appears dozens of times in the Bible. But what does it mean? The "fear of the Lord" is very often misunderstood. The word "fear" is derived from the Hebrew word *yir'ah* which means fear, terror. But it also has a moral connotation of reverence. We often make the mistake of swinging to extremes when it comes to understanding the fear of the Lord. We tend to define it as meaning that God can punish us with hell—so we better not cross Him. Or we might think that we must stand in great reverence and in awe of Him. (We need to do both.)

Mankind needs to have an acute awareness of the reality of hell and understand that God *does* punish sin. But we cannot walk around fearing that God is watching us and is ready to pounce on us for any slight indiscretion. Nevertheless, we must fear the Lord in reverence. We know fire can be very destructive but it can also bless us with the usefulness of heat and light. In a similar way, we must also understand *who* God is and exactly how *powerful* He is.

Perhaps a more appropriate analogy would be that of a child who has the fear of his father. My young children do not live in a state of fear around me. But they do understand that as their father, I have a God-given authority over them. My young sons know that if I give them "the look" they should stop what they are doing immediately or there will be consequences. I have to punish any wrongdoings but they also know how much I love them. It is that love that motivates them to want to please me.

The fear of the Lord is most appropriately expressed in individuals who understand who they are in relation to God, and stand in awe of who He is. They understand their own sinfulness. It makes perfect sense that since God is the Source of wisdom we must come to Him on the basis of "the fear of the Lord." The fear of the Lord is necessary for living a successful Christian life; it accentuates a hatred for sin. Proverbs 8:13a states, "The fear of the LORD is to hate evil." Furthermore, it is the fear of the Lord that motivates a person toward repentance. Proverbs 16:6b declares "…by the fear of the LORD *men* depart from evil."

The fear of the Lord is also connected to an obedient Christian life of holiness. In Ecclesiastes 12:13-14, the Preacher (traditionally taken to be Solomon) writes, "Let us hear the conclusion of the entire matter: Fear God, and keep his commandments: for this *is* the whole *duty* of man. For God shall bring every work into judgment, with every secret thing, whether *it be* good, or whether *it be* evil."

An obvious connection exists between fearing God and keeping His commandments (stemming from an understanding of our accountability to God for our actions). We cannot hope to live a blessed life without first grasping the fear of the Lord. God offers intimacy to those who fear Him. Psalm 25:14 reveals, "The secret of the LORD *is* with them that fear him; and he will shew them his covenant." (This intimacy comes in the form of illumination.)

When we fear the Lord—the Holy Spirit will open our eyes to behold wondrous things described within the pages of Scripture. Connecting the dots in Scripture as to *how* we choose to live our lives is most certainly walking in wisdom.

FEAR IS CONTAGIOUS

For some reason one of my children has struggled with a fear of dogs. If someone even says the word "dog" he will panic. He demonstrates his fear in various ways. He may begin to shout, climb up on chairs or tables—or try to climb up into my arms or my wife's arms. He may even run for safety and scream all along the way.

In the process of this spectacle sometimes his younger brother (who actually loves dogs), will get caught-up in his brother's emotion and start to be afraid. He doesn't know what he's afraid of, he just knows that his brother is afraid and so he becomes afraid. Fear is contagious. In the Hebrew camp, fear spread from ten spies to millions of Israelis instantly (Numbers 13:31-14:1).

While we certainly don't want to spread irrational fear, if we are to inspire others to embark on the journey toward wisdom—we do want to spread a fear of the Lord. This is the job of Christian leaders whether in church, at home or in the workplace. In Ezekiel 44:23 we find that leaders are to "…teach my people *the difference* between the holy and profane, and cause them to discern between the unclean and the clean." There is a right way and wrong way to go about inspiring the fear of the Lord.

Fear That Is Caught—Not Taught

"Wherefore the Lord said, Forasmuch as this people draw near me with their mouth, and with their lips do honour me, but have removed their heart far from me, and their fear toward me is taught by the precept of men" (Isaiah 29:13).

The phrase "taught" in this passage is quite interesting. It is derived from the Hebrew word *lâmad* and means properly to *goad, i.e. by implication to teach.* It is intended to arouse the image of a farmer goading his oxen as he plows his field. Before tractors, farmers plowed the fields with a mighty ox yoked to a hand-guided plow. Farmers always want to plow straight rows and since oxen do not come with steering wheels a method had to be formulated to keep them in line.

Enter the ox goad. An ox goad is in its essence a long stick with a sharp point or hook. When the ox would venture to one side the farmer would take the stick and jab it into the backside of the ox giving it the message that it needed to straighten out. The farmer would spend his day poking the ox with a goad to make sure it went the way it should go.

A powerful word picture is described in Isaiah 29:13. The fear of God was taught by the precepts of men. In other words, the only reason people were doing what they were supposed to be doing was because someone was goading them along and making them do it. Some families have this experience on Sunday mornings. Mom or dad walk into the teenager's bedroom and goad the son or daughter out of bed. This is followed by goading the teen into getting dressed, eating breakfast and getting into the car to go to church. In other words, the motivation for what the teen is being told to do is not a heartfelt desire to honor God, but rather a forced situation.

Adults also often find themselves in a similar position. The only reason they put something in the basket on Sunday is because they don't want anyone to look at them and think that they aren't doing what they are supposed to. It's not a true fear of the Lord motivating their obedience, it's a fear that is taught by the precepts of men. The only way some people will do the right thing is to have someone make them do it. The problem with fear that is taught by the precepts of men is that it produces Pharisees. In the book of Mark, Jesus is quoted giving a description of the Pharisees:

"He answered and said unto them, 'Well hath Esaias prophesied of you hypocrites, as it is written, This people honoureth me with *their* lips, but their heart is far from me. Howbeit in vain do they worship me, teaching *for* doctrines the commandments of men. For laying aside the commandment of God, ye hold the tradition of men, *as* the washing of pots and cups: and many other such like things ye do.' And he said unto them, 'Full well ye reject the commandment of God, that ye may keep your own tradition'" (Mark 7:6-9).

The greatest crime of the Pharisees was that they elevated the tradition of men to an equal, and at times—greater status than the Word of God. Traditions of men do not produce a true fear of the Lord that leads to wisdom. Traditions of men lead people toward legalism. Too many churches exist wherein the leader goes around goading the members into following a set of prescribed rules: Dress like this, talk like this, don't participate in this but do participate in that, etc. God never intended a pastor to be a farmer with a goad prodding his congregation. The pastor is to be a shepherd leading his congregation. The people follow the pastor as *he* follows Christ.

If someone has to make you honor God, you have a fear that is taught. That kind of fear would place a person on the same level as a hypocritical Pharisee. The passage in Isaiah 29:13 about fear that is taught by the precepts of men speaks to two groups. First, to those who are not genuine in their relationship with God. Second, it also speaks to those who are teaching the fear of the Lord. Rather than fear that is taught by the ideologies of men, we need to learn to inspire a true fear of the Lord that leads others to wisdom—not hypocrisy.

The true teaching of the fear of the Lord is perhaps most essential in the home. Statistics show that two out of three young people will become disengaged from their faith after they graduate high school. Tragically, large numbers of youth are leaving the Church veering off into the foolishness of secular humanism and into what Spurgeon called "practical atheism" (saying there is a God, but living as if He doesn't exist).

How can we teach our young people to fear the Lord? We certainly don't want to produce Pharisees, but we do want to instill into our children a genuine fear of the Lord; a fear that is caught not a fear that is taught. To accomplish that goal the "law of the home" is very much needed.

THE LAW OF THE HOME

"My son, hear the instruction of thy father, and forsake not the law of thy mother: For they shall be an ornament of grace unto thy head, and chains about thy neck" (Proverbs 1:8-9).

The book of Proverbs gives us guidelines on how to instill and promote the fear of the Lord in the home. I like to call it the "law of the home." The law of the home consists of the rules of the home that the parents establish. In order for a household to operate properly, parents must establish rules and practices.

These directives function to support the accomplishment of the goals of the home. If the parents desire is to promote wisdom, then they need to purposely establish a law of the home that will aid in instilling a fear of the Lord. According to Proverbs 2:1-5 the purpose of the law of the home is to *understand* the fear of the Lord.

> "My son, if thou wilt receive my words, and hide my commandments with thee; So that thou incline thine ear unto wisdom, *and* apply thine heart to understanding; Yea, if thou criest after knowledge, *and* liftest up thy voice for understanding; If thou seekest her as silver, and searchest for her as *for* hid treasures; **then shalt thou understand the fear of the LORD, and find the knowledge of God.**" [emphasis added]

The law of the home is not a rod for beating children into submission or even a cookie cutter method to produce a certain type of child. It is a conscious effort on the part of parents to communicate to the child that God *is* the priority of the home and His ways take precedence *over* everything else. It is the parent echoing the words of Joshua 24:15 "...but as for me and my house, we will serve the LORD." The law of the home translates these words into specific acts of devotion which demonstrate that commitment.

Consistently, throughout the book of Proverbs young people are instructed to embrace the rules set in place by their parents. Some see the law of the home as a nuisance to be rejected. Television and movies directed at children and youth repeatedly contain the blatant message that the rules and instructions of parents should be rejected. Frequently the plots of these programs contain instances in which children disregard or disobey their parents to do what they believe is "right in their hearts." Rebellious actions of children are portrayed as acceptable without accountability or uncomfortable consequences.

More often than not, it is the parents who foolishly give in and come around to the child's way of thinking and acting. After all, "a little child shall lead them." These dynamics are nothing less than demonically inspired propaganda continually emanating from Hollywood—seeking to undermine the influence of godly authority. God's plan is for children to respect and accept the instruction and rules of their parents. The children who do so develop a fear of the Lord and are on the path to wisdom. The challenge for parents is to make the law of the home seem like fine jewelry to be worn by their children with pride, rather than a nuisance to be rejected.

When I was a young boy of about ten years old I attended a Christian school that was planning a trip to the circus. Everyone at the school was very excited when the opportunity to go to the event was announced. But when my parents learned about the trip they were not pleased. After seeing some advertisements for the circus they told me and my younger sister that they had decided not to let us go. (The circus actors were wearing immodest clothing and my parents felt it would be inappropriate for us to take part in the trip.)

> Secular education is filled with humanistic philosophies promoting evil, all with an evolutionary foundation.

Of course when the other students heard I was not going I had to explain why. They were not very understanding and mocked me for quite some time—especially the older boys. I missed out on the circus but I don't remember feeling any regret, even though I was mocked. My parents were taking a stand for God by expressing the law of the home. I didn't like it but I understood what they were doing. I wore that teaching like a badge of fine jewelry—a badge of honor unto the Lord.

So many Christian families today are in need of the law of the home. Parents must set practical standards and give their children biblical reasons for what they are doing. Godly standards serve as guardrails along the path of life—pointing children to a fear of the Lord. Establishing boundaries also creates an environment in the home that demonstrates God as the priority and effectively encourages the principal pursuit of wisdom.

My wife does a masterful job of explaining the law of the home to our daughter in the area of modesty. We have established standards in our home to promote modesty in dress. She tells our daughter to dress first in a way that honors God and also in a way that shows respect to herself and to those around her. Now we know that we cannot point to any particular verse in the Bible that says how long a skirt should be or at what point on the shoulders the shirt should cover. Regardless, we have established standards or landmarks which point her in the direction that puts God first in every area—including clothing choices.

When our daughter is old enough to be on her own she may decide to adjust those guidelines a bit and that's okay. The law of the home is based on godly principals and not intended to make a child feel like an object of a farmer's goading. The purpose is to make the home a place for promoting righteousness and holiness in fear of the Lord.

I believe that there is a biblical mandate to go one step beyond the law of the home by ensuring that the instruction the children receive outside the home is based on a fear of the Lord. When a child has the law of the home in place pointing them to the fear of the Lord, it is also imperative that the school point them in the same direction.

Secular education is filled with humanistic philosophies promoting evil, all with an evolutionary foundation. It is the antithesis of the fear of the Lord. Don't allow the law of the home to be undermined five days a week for over thirty hours. If Jesus is not allowed in the classroom then my children will not be there either. Homeschooling and good Christian schools are essential tools for families in order to lead their children to wisdom.

Why is the law of the home and ensuring that it is not undermined so important? Because that is how God can capture the attention of children. The epidemic of young people in the United States abandoning the faith is not just a bunch of statistics. It hits home in every church and every family. Sure, every individual must decide for oneself and the Garden of Eden is proof that even a perfect environment cannot guarantee preservation, but the stakes are too high for parents not to have a protective strategy.

When the words and commandments of the parents (the law of the home) are embraced by the child it produces an understanding of the fear of the Lord. This is the ultimate goal of the law of the home; it is not about regimented conformity—that's goading. Creating an awareness and understanding of how important the fear of the Lord actually is, should be a priority for parents when relating to their children.

I love the Dr. Seuss classic, *Green Eggs and Ham.* The entire premise of the book is that the unnamed character does not like green eggs and ham. But the character Sam-I-Am is persistent in trying everything he can to get that unnamed character to try them. The unnamed character rejects eating the food until he cannot take the persistent prodding any longer. He tells Sam-I-Am that he will try the green eggs and ham if he will stop pestering him. So he tries the food and to his great surprise finds that he does indeed like what he had so persistently rejected.

So many people have never tasted and seen for themselves that the Lord is loving and good. The law of the home brings an understanding of how good the fear of the Lord is and encourages the child to taste and see this for themselves. The ultimate goal is to have a fear that is *caught rather than taught*. To be effective, the law of the home must function consistently, always encouraging the child to embrace the fear of the Lord. The law of the home is the best tool for parents. It is much more than a set of rules that lead their children to wisdom. It is a broad-based strategy parents can implement to combat negative worldly influences.

Whether it is prioritizing church attendance, restricting certain media or dealing with a host of other areas, the focus for parents (and leaders) must be singular—minimizing the pull of the ungodly while maximizing the value of the fear of the Lord. If the law of the home only seeks to minimize evil it will either be rejected or create a Pharisee. The law of the home must first seek to lovingly instill the fear of the Lord. In the pursuit of wisdom, the fear of the Lord is where it all begins. When the fear of the Lord is the starting point, "You CAN get there from here."

THE LAW OF THE HOME APPLIED
The law of the home is not intended to be a stick to beat out behaviors but rather to serve as a guide for the heart condition. When behavior is the focus, the direction of the heart can be lost and produce a Pharisee. Here are a few questions to consider in guiding the implementation of the law of the home:

- Am I equating my law of the home to Scripture? The answer will be evident if I think my children have sinned because they broke the law of the home rather than realizing the real sin is in the violation of the Fifth Commandment to honor parents.

51

- Am I creating this law to promote my own authority or does it have a deeper purpose to help my children understand the fear of the Lord? This will be evident if I am more offended by the fact that they have gone against "my rules and standards" rather than viewing such a situation as their relationship with the Lord as weak.

- Does the punishment fit the crime? Every time the law of the home is broken there must be consequences. Obviously, levels of consequences need to be based on individual circumstances. Using a bazooka for every little offense will not have the desired effect of bringing about an understanding of the fear of the Lord. I have learned that starting at a level 10 with the volume of my voice leaves me with nowhere to go. If one of my children leave a toy in the living room it will not be effective to yell, berate, spank and ground. Save the "big guns" for when they are needed.

Asking the type of questions I have suggested can help bring focus and clarity to the application of the law of the home. It can help avoid the pitfall of becoming a Pharisee who is only concerned with the conformity of behavior. The ultimate objective of the law of the home is to point children to a fear of the Lord. While the conformity of behavior makes us feel good in the immediate short-term, the long-term goal is achieving wisdom. (That is the difference between a fear that is taught and a fear that is caught.)

The Law of Forgiveness
"But there is forgiveness with thee, that thou mayest be feared" (Psalm 130:4). When we realize the great depths of forgiveness that God extends to us we have yet another reason to stand in awe of Him (fear God). Consequences bring about a realization of sinfulness which in and of itself can tend to make one feel inadequate, lowly and even depressed. This is not the purpose of the law of the home. To counter this, forgiveness must be freely extended.

When a realization of a wrongdoing has occurred and feelings of remorse abound—the extension of forgiveness is powerful medicine. When there has been a problem and following the administration of punishment, my children almost immediately say, "I'm sorry, do you forgive me?" (This is the desired response.) My wife and I then immediately grant that request. If our children don't automatically ask for forgiveness in a situation we will prompt them to do so. By doing this the effectiveness of the law of the home remains strong.

When children realize that their offense was egregious and that they deserve punishment, but then quickly receive forgiveness—the parent models to their children the relationship God desires to have with them. Our sin demands judgment and condemnation, but God offers forgiveness. Children will stand in awe (fear) of this amazing grace offered to them.

The power of forgiveness extends both ways. Parents cannot be so arrogant as to think that they can do no wrong. They will make mistakes and when they do, they must seek forgiveness from the child. This puts the child in the position of being able to model the forgiveness that God offers. This is powerful for them to experience and will further aid in understanding the fear of the Lord and point them toward gaining an understanding of wisdom.

Points to Ponder

- Do you fear God?
- Is your fear taught by the precepts of men?
- Do you have a law in the home and does that law promote the fear of the Lord?
- Are you helping your family members get off on the right foot to begin their journey to wisdom?

Part Three

The Roadmap

Chapter Eight

⚓

The Five Travelers

A N AGE-OLD DEBATE has plagued one generation after another. It is centered around the assertion that "men are better drivers than women." This battle of the sexes can be argued with great intensity and the debate can be spirited at times, to say the least. So the stereotype is more myth than fact. Studies have shown that men are more confident drivers, but that the ladies are more cautious. What do the statistics reveal? Sorry, guys, but the data shows that even after accounting for the fact that men drive 30 percent more than women, they are responsible for more accidents than the ladies.

So often, there are stereotypes that influence the lens through which others are viewed. The problem with stereotypes is that they are often very wrong. Stereotypes can lead to prejudicial perceptions of others and for the most part—should be avoided. Belonging to a certain ethnic group or being a particular gender is not a predetermination to act a certain way. This sort of biased perspective is often referred to in the Scriptures as being a "respecter of persons."

While the focal point of the book of Proverbs is to cultivate a relationship with God, the overall message examines human relationships. Proverbs has a description of every type of person; many types of travelers are described in the book of Proverbs. Often they are described in contrast to one another.

The righteous are contrasted with the wicked. The sluggard or slothful is contrasted with the diligent. The wise with the fool, etc. These contrasts are not only poetic expressions, they are also very useful descriptive ways in which to recognize personality types. Sometimes the best way to understand a concept or idea is to understand what it is not. Contrast can help bring about that understanding.

Let's take Proverbs chapter fifteen as an example. The overall purpose of that chapter is to contrast the wicked and the righteous. Out of thirty-three verses in that chapter, twenty-four of them utilize the poetic expression of contrast. The wicked and righteous are described in polar opposite extremes. The consequences of wickedness are brutal, but the blessings of righteousness are enormous. These contrasts assist the reader in understanding the messages in the text. The first verse of the chapter is often quoted and because of the presentation of the extreme contrast, a clear visualization and understanding is brought to the reader's mind. "A soft answer turneth away wrath: but grievous words stir up anger." These contrasts are helpful in that from them emerge five distinct and clear types of travelers or character types found in the book of Proverbs. These are personifications, not stereotypes.

These five characterizations describe the conduct and behavior of individuals in general. Every individual can be identified within one of these characterizations. They are the Simple, the Scorner, the Fool, the Prudent, and the Wise. These terms, as used in Proverbs do not describe one particular behavior, but rather a pattern of behaviors as demonstrated by an individual. One person is referred to as "simple" because he exhibits a certain set of characteristics, and another is a "fool" because of his particular behaviors, etc.

In high school I was first introduced to psychology when we studied the four personality types: Choleric, sanguine, phlegmatic and melancholy. I can remember studying them and then trying to pin myself and everyone in my family with the right label. I find such studies to be fascinating and useful in understanding how to better relate to certain types of people.

The five character types in Proverbs are not a psychological analysis of any personality type. A sanguine can be simple, a scorner, a fool, prudent or wise. The book of Proverbs offers a spiritual analysis that indicates the status and direction of a person's life. Proverbs uses the five characteristics like marks on a map indicating position and direction—with the wise and fool demonstrating opposite extremes. Of course, the ultimate objective of life's journey is to attain wisdom. It is the principal pursuit with all that it entails. We know that not everyone is traveling in the same direction and there are forces at work to pull at some and move them in a certain direction (good or bad).

An examination of each of the characterizations portrayed in the book of Proverbs is useful both individually and relationally. Individually, it is helpful to pinpoint one's location in respect to wisdom. If an honest evaluation of spiritual status reveals anything less than wisdom, a course correction should be pursued. Relationally, being aware of the various character types is helpful in understanding the spiritual status of others. Since the journey to wisdom requires leadership, it benefits the leader to know from where they are leading others. Specific steps and processes are described in Proverbs which are most helpful and successful when dealing with each of the five personality types.

It is important to see the five personality types in the book of Proverbs not just as individuals located on a map, but as interconnected personalities. A road that exists in and of itself with no entrance or exit, but totally isolated is an anomaly. There must always be a connection from one road to another for any sort of meaningful transportation to occur. Resist the temptation to see the five character types on separate roads without any interconnections. Take a step back, take some time to study a map overview. An overview of the five personality types of Proverbs will enable Christian leaders, in particular, to not only identify the location of an individual on the roadmap, but also assist in preparing a strategy for guiding them to what should be their ultimate destination—godly wisdom. Awareness of a few key patterns and stages will greatly assist with this endeavor.

Everyone starts life as a simple person. This fact in and of itself underscores the values of those years and the shaping influence it has upon the life of the child and the direction in which he or she will ultimately travel. Significant effort and resources need to be invested into this early stage of life to help guide the individual toward wisdom and away from foolishness. Research indicates that the first five years of a child's development are vital and can have ramifications (both positive and negative) for decades. The simple are indeed at the staging ground of life. As they progress in years they will approach a fork in the road where they will be required to make a decision as to which direction to take. The influences and experiences of the simple will all calculate into that very pivotal decision.

As the simple approach their tween years (ages 10-12) and early teen years, they will begin to indicate what direction they are headed. This is the beginning point for choosing to be scornful or prudent. As they grow older in their teen years and young adult years a definite direction will be evidenced. They will be traveling toward the direction of fools or toward the direction of the wise. For some it will be blatant. For others it will be more subtle. Perhaps it will seem as though some are parked on the breakdown lane on the roadmap of life near the scorner. They aren't quite out and out fools, but they carry the attitude of a scorner. Still others may decide to stop at the road of prudence. They demonstrate maturity and leadership, but they don't have the desire to go on to wisdom. (Be sure to keep the map overview in mind during any personal examination as well as in considerations for leadership.) The location of a person determines the direction he or she needs to pursue.

All of these roads on the journey are connected. An individual may be far removed from wisdom and headed down the path of fools, yet he or she can always make a U-turn and find the road to wisdom. Remember, the current status of an individual is not a life sentence without the ability to make changes and improvements. No one is born to be a fool or scorner. Wisdom is always available. Anyone who is willing to backtrack (repent) and embrace the fear of the Lord can find a fresh starting point to travel toward wisdom.

On the journey to wisdom, the locations on the map are all interconnected. Keep the entirety of the roadmap in mind, not only for individual success but also for the development of successful strategies when leading others.

Points to Ponder

- Am I guilty of being a "respecter of persons" through inappropriate stereotyping?

- Am I prepared to honestly examine myself and those whom I love in light of the biblical characterizations of the five character types described in Proverbs?

Chapter Nine

⚓

A Simple Start

O ye simple, understand wisdom:..
Proverbs 8:5a

ONE SPRING DAY as a young boy of about eleven years old, I was walking in the woods alongside our home while playing with a stick. (When I was growing up sticks were one of my favorite toys.) I could be anything in my imagination as I battled against pirates, climbed the highest mountain, parted the sea or lead an army into battle. During this particular saunter in the woods my little curly-haired sister had decided to tag along. She was about four years old and was holding her doll and her special blankie as she trudged behind her big brother. I would normally fulfill my big brother duty of resisting and not allow her to tag along, but she was being quiet so I didn't mind.

As I walked along with my stick I did what any red-blooded boy would do. I hit trees with it. However, the stick was a lot weaker than I anticipated and after a solid whack, the stick broke into many pieces flying in all directions. One of the pieces flew exactly in the direction of my little sister and struck her in the face! I saw it happen and felt really badly about it. I immediately went to check on her but her response was instantaneous, almost instinctive, as she made a beeline straight for the back door of our house. As she ran she was crying out, "Mom! Dad! Adam hit me with a stick!"

I began to panic a bit as I worried about the potential consequences. (It's amazing how many scenarios one can imagine in a short period of time.) I knew that I hadn't "technically" hit her with a stick, but that I had acted recklessly and it was my fault that she was hurt. I finally decided on blaming the tree as my defense. Thankfully, the damage wasn't severe and she was just fine. After my parents had addressed their injured little one my father turned his attention to me. He asked me what had happened, but I could see fire in his eyes as he stared at me. I swallowed hard and proceeded to carefully explain the situation giving meticulous attention to the role that the tree played being sure to lay all blame at its roots.

My father listened carefully. As he began to realize that it was genuinely an accident the fire began to diminish from his eyes, which was a tremendous relief for me. He didn't yell at me or punish me in any way that day, but he said something I've never forgotten; something that has been very formative in my life. He looked at me and said, "I need you to be mature. Mature means *thinking before* you act. Before you do something think to yourself, *If I do this what will happen?* Be mature and think ahead." I had acted very immaturely and instead of just addressing a particular instance, my father, in his wisdom, was providing direction for my life. I was that character that Proverbs refers to as the "simple" and he was directing me away from its immaturity toward the maturity of prudence and wisdom.

THE SIMPLE DEFINED

The first of the five character types in the book of Proverbs that we must understand is the "simple." Proverbs chapter seven is dedicated to the instruction of the "simple ones." The term "simple" is often associated with youth in Proverbs (1:4 and 7:7). It is also characterized by naivety and immaturity. Everyone starts out life as a simple person. This is not a bad thing. It just means that all children are "simple" because they lack knowledge and experience.

It is the simple who "believe every word" according to Proverbs 14:15. Perhaps this is why the Lord instructed us to become as a "little child" in regard to our faith. We must simply take Him at His Word. Children will simply believe what they are told—even wild fantasy's that defy logic and reason. Characters like Santa Clause, the Easter Bunny, and the Tooth Fairy are for children. They are simple, and naivety is one of their predominant characteristics.

GUIDING THE SIMPLE

Because of their gullibility and inability to analyze a situation maturely, the simple can be easily influenced and fall prey to wickedness. Great care must be taken in the selection of those who are allowed to hold a position of influence in their lives. For this reason, over and over again in the Scriptures—the warning is given to stay away from those who would lead the simple to error. Do not enter into the path of the wicked but rather pursue righteousness in the way of wisdom.

One of the most powerful forces in a young person's life is peer pressure. So many succumb to the relentless bullying of their peers and become involved in harmful, often dangerous situations. This is why the guidance of parents is so important for the simple. That picture of parental guidance is illustrated for us in Proverbs 1:10-19, as the father and mother instruct their son to refrain his foot from the path of sinners. Sadly, the path to wisdom is littered with what is left of so many simple ones after the wicked have gotten hold of them (Proverbs 1:32). Since the simple will believe nearly anything and are prone to follow anyone, they need to be safeguarded and guided into truth. They need the opportunity to develop discernment through maturity, which requires proper guidance.

Modern technology presents many challenges regarding the safety and well-being of our children. It is no longer uncommon for very young children to have a cell phone with the potential for accessing the Internet. While this may open a wealth of information for them it can also be like opening Pandora's box. Ungodly unwholesome images and ideas can flash across the screen robbing children of their innocence. What is perhaps an even greater threat is the tremendous potential for planting thoughts that will lead to embracing worldly philosophies.

Nielson Holdings, a global information data and measurement company reports that American children between the ages of two and eighteen years old spend 28-32 hours per week in front of the television. Disney, Nickelodeon and PBS Kids play a major role in shaping the thought processes of the simple, and much of it is contrary to Scripture and leads children away from godly wisdom. The media lead the simple to the way of fools when they say things like, "Follow your heart" (Proverbs 28:26).

Immoral agendas are being blatantly promoted to young children in cartoons and popular programs. In this deteriorating culture, sexuality is no longer a taboo subject for our very young age children. Parents need to be aware of what their children are watching, where they are surfing on the Internet and capitalize on the advantages of using protective software. But we can only protect them for so long. It is essential that parents and other godly influences in the lives of the simple will equip them to be discerning in these areas.

Carl Kerby, in a presentation for the apologetics course titled "Demolishing Strongholds" (published by Answers in Genesis, an apologetics ministry), proposed a powerful concept that will help the simple. He is a former FAA flight controller and he used the analogy of getting young people to "turn their radar on." Truly there exists a plethora of philosophies and teachings in the media that are poisonous to the simple and pull against the way of wisdom. Avoiding it altogether is close to impossible, but as Carl Kirby says, "If you're not recognizing it you're absorbing it."

More than once while watching a movie with my young children I have interrupted it and said, "That's not true! God's Word says…" I am trying to teach them to turn on their radar and move from the gullibility and immaturity of simplicity toward wisdom. It blesses me when I hear my children audibly scold a program they are watching for promoting something that is contrary to the Word of God. I am encouraged to know that their radar is on and they are beginning to test things against the Word of God. "A prudent man foreseeth the evil, and hideth himself: but the simple *pass on*, and are punished" (Proverbs 22:3).

Because the simple can be so precarious they are in desperate need for the law of the home which is the key to the shaping of the simple. The entire purpose of the law of the home is to protect the simple and give them a fighting chance to start on the path toward wisdom at an early age. Parents must ensure that there is a law in their home that it is encouraging positive growth in their little ones.

The law of the home is under significant attack in our culture, primarily due to the demise of marriage and the nuclear family. The Center for Disease Control has documented that over 40 percent of all live births in the United States have been reported to be out of wedlock. The trend is that this will be even higher in the future. A John Hopkins University study shows that a startling 57 percent of millennials are having children out of wedlock.

Yale University's publication, *YaleGlobal Online*, reports that the trend is occurring worldwide with an uptick of out of wedlock births around the world. The absence of both parents in a committed marriage relationship leaves the simple at a disadvantage right out of the gate. The statistics on the effects of fatherlessness are stunning; there is no question that the breakdown of the family is a significant contributor to the carnage that the simple are experiencing.

Just because the family is broken in our culture does not mean that there is no hope for the simple. Something significant the simple can do for themselves is heed instruction as portrayed over and over again in the book of Proverbs. Regardless of their home situation, if the simple receive positive instruction they can avoid many pitfalls and position themselves in the direction of wisdom. This truth is confirmed by the many testimonies of disadvantaged youth that point to a teacher or mentor that helped them get through their rough times.

The simple are at the crossroads of life. In one direction they can hear wisdom calling, but in the other—the seductive trap of folly beckons. The simple need special attention and confident leadership to guide them toward wisdom.

God Takes Special Interest in the Simple

God takes a special interest in the simple. The song, "Jesus Loves the Little Children" is not just a quaint children's song, it reflects a special message which Jesus consistently proclaimed in the Scriptures. Jesus boldly rebuked his disciples when they would not allow the little children to approach Him. His order to "forbid them not" also included the powerful commentary, "For of such is the kingdom of heaven" (Matthew 19:14). The simple suffer from a lack of attention much too often, but never at the hand of the Lord Jesus.

The Old Testament contains many Scripture references to the pagan false god, Molech. It is almost always in the context of giving children or causing those children to pass through the fire. The horrific practices of worshipping this false god included sacrificing children. God expressly forbade His people from partaking in that ritual and punished them when they did. This barbaric practice has its modern day equivalent in the genocide of abortion that is occurring all around the world. So many misguided politicians and activists are encouraging the slaughter of millions of unborn children. They are sacrificing the simple on the altar of convenience. God is not interested in sacrificing the simple. He is dedicated to preserving them: "The LORD preserveth the simple" (Psalm 116:6).

The highly respected Barna Group has reported that the simple provide the greatest opportunity for evangelism. Two out of three born-again Christians made their commitment to Christ before reaching the age of 18. However, the research also further discovered that 43 percent of all born-again Christians came to saving faith before the age of 13. The demographic of the simple is the greatest opportunity for the Church to fulfill the Great Commission.

I can certainly testify to the accuracy of this study by my own experience. I can still recall in vivid detail when I first made a confession of Christ as my Savior and exercised saving faith. I was the ripe old age of three. I had been going to church for nine months before I was born and my parents were faithful to teach me God's ways at home and bring me to church weekly. At the age of three, I began to feel convicted of my sins and asked my mother to pray with me for salvation. I shared a room with my older brother; we had bunk beds. Together she and I knelt by the bottom bunk and I repented of my sins and asked Jesus to be my Savior.

One of my first church responsibilities upon graduation from Bible college was that of a youth pastor, ministering to those who were as young as five up to age eighteen. On two separate occasions I have been blessed by the testimonies of seniors graduating from high school when relating their salvation experience. Both of them recalled a time before they turned the age of twelve and were led to the Lord as a direct result of my youth ministry. I carry around in my wallet a copy of a high school writing assignment completed by one of those students. In it she relates one particular instance where she was challenged to accept Christ as her Savior. This is what she had to say:

> When I was five my Sunday school teacher, Mr. Rondeau, told us about salvation. He told us we were all sinners and the only way to get to heaven was to ask Jesus to come into our hearts. He also told us that Jesus loves us and wants us to accept Him and live for Him. Then he asked if anyone wanted to accept Jesus into his or her heart, to kneel by their seat and repeat the prayer after him. So I got down on my knees and asked Jesus into my heart. I was so excited to be saved. I hope one day my testimony of how I got saved will touch others and encourage them to ask Jesus to save them too.

We know there are those who are skeptical about children getting saved. They worry that they are not genuinely being saved, but rather being led to repeat a "hocus pocus prayer." While this is not an illegitimate concern in some instances, there is certainly a danger in "throwing the baby out with the bathwater." Children represent the greatest opportunity for the Church to successfully fulfill the Great Commission. How illogical it would be for the Church to ignore the ministry of the life-changing message to that special group. After all, their greatest opportunity for growing from simple to wise is to begin with salvation. The great lyrics penned by Clare Herbert Woolston in the classic song "Jesus Loves the Little Children" has expressed that sentiment for over a century:

> Jesus loves the little children.
> All the children of the world.
> Red, brown, yellow
> Black and white.
> They are precious in His sight.
> Jesus love the little children
> Of the world.

I am fascinated by the recruitment and vetting process that many local congregations employ when searching for a new pastor. Resumes are carefully examined. Detailed questionnaires are completed and analyzed by a carefully selected committee. Interviews are conducted with family and references are thoroughly checked.

The local church may even take a test drive one Sunday and kick the tires on a person's preaching skills. Careful and meticulous steps are taken to ensure that the right person with all the scriptural qualifications and the clear call of God on his life is selected. This is right and proper and careful vetting is important. But I am flabbergasted that so many churches have such poor vetting techniques when it comes to finding leaders to fulfill the role of the youth minister.

Far too often the only questions asked sound something like, "Can you breathe?" And, "Are you willing to help out?" If this is the whitest field of the harvest wouldn't it make the most sense to take special care for the evangelism and discipleship of this target group? If God takes such special interest in the simple, then so should every local church.

Nursery and kid's church should not be drudge ministries that only serve to get the kids out of the way so the adults can have quiet. Yet far too many church leaders view it exactly that way. As I stated earlier, when I started out in fulltime ministry after graduating from Bible college, my first major assignment was to take charge of the children's church. It was lacking in several areas and needed significant development. I was not going to be a babysitter.

I immediately began to set about creating a program and sought to make it the highlight of the week for the kids. It was a lot of fun and exciting with songs, puppets, skits, object lessons, games and a snack (by far the favorite of many). I was the pastor of those children and each week I prepared a sermon for them. It wasn't like the sermons for the adults in the big people sanctuary; after all, we're talking about very young children. My sermons were tailored to meet their needs. Over a span of four years I had developed a curriculum that took the children through the Scriptures chronologically—all the while incorporating salvation, sound doctrine and a biblical worldview. I even developed a ten-week series on eschatology. The kids loved it and would beg their parents to bring them to church because they didn't want to miss children's church.

That ministry wasn't just for fun. Salvations were happening and discipleship was taking place; the entire church profited as a whole. Serving the simple should not be a necessary evil. It should be an integral joyful element of the ministry of every church. The forms of implementation may vary from church to church, but the need to minister to the very young remains constant.

THE NEEDS OF THE SIMPLE

The greatest need of the simple is to be regularly exposed to God's Word. It is the Scriptures that can make the simple wise. Psalm 19:7 states, "The law of the Lord is perfect converting the soul: the testimony of the Lord is sure, making wise the simple." The only hope for the simple, in fact, is that they receive instruction from this Book of books. "The entrance of thy words giveth light; it giveth understanding unto the simple" (Psalm 119:130).

Christian leaders (with emphasis upon parents) must strive to saturate young people with the Word of God through whatever means possible. The Word of God is the young person's primary source of attaining wisdom and avoiding folly. Those very same Scriptures are under intense attack in our culture. In particular, secular education and the media are constantly attempting to undermine the validity of the Scriptures and train students instead to view life through the lens of secular humanism.

The devil is strategic and tactical in his approach. He knows that it is the Word of God that will keep the simple from his traps of folly and give them a fighting chance at wisdom. The great challenge of modern Christian leadership is to successfully defend the Christian faith through apologetics.

Pollster Brit Beemer has compiled some fascinating statistics on the state of the Christian faith in the United States, with a particular emphasis upon youth. In the book *Already Gone,* he, along with Ken Ham, founder and president of the apologetics ministry, Answers in Genesis, provide a compelling analysis as to why young people are abandoning the faith. They state, "We forget that the first attack by Satan was to cast doubt on the Word of God." The two men arrive at the compelling conclusion that the reason so many young people are abandoning the faith is because they reject the authority of Scripture.

When the Scriptures are undermined by the culture at large without providing an adequate defense, doubts will arise in the minds of the simple. Authors, Ken Ham and Brit Beemer conclude, "We need to defend the Word of God as one of our top priorities as Christians. If we are to give a strategic and effective response to the wave of souls who are leaving the Church, these issues must be addressed."

> The greatest need of the simple is to be regularly exposed to God's Word.

There comes a time in the lives of children when they begin to expand their thinking. They no longer believe that a fat man in a red suit squeezes down the chimney, leaves presents under the tree, has a quick snack and then scales back up the skinny chimney. They are still simple, but they are coming to a crossroads. They are beginning to mature and think logically. At this point, they will have a lot of questions as their thinking processes begin to form. The simple are seeking answers. If parents and godly leaders don't give the answers, the world will, and will drive them away from God.

In John Bunyan's classic *The Pilgrim's Progress*, the main character, Christian, very early in his journey comes into contact with Mr. Worldly Wiseman. He, through his fair speech and logic, persuades Christian to leave the Way that the Book and Evangelist have shown him. Christian does this to his own detriment until Evangelist finds him and reassures his faith in the Book and his directions. This analogy was first published in 1678 and is still evident today.

The world is indeed seeking to turn the simple away from the way of wisdom onto the path of fools, which leads to destruction. This is done by providing the simple with answers to their questions that undermine the Scriptures— leading them away from the truth. Are Christian leaders effectively countering that with solid answers from God's Word? The statistics seem to be saying that in many instances they are not.

Parents and church leaders must be ready to answer the questions that young people have about the faith. It's not just teens asking them either. In many cases, it's the tweens and younger children. When I was a young boy of preschool age I asked my father a very spiritual question that my little brain had contrived. I looked at him and said, "Hey, Dad. How does God have a Son, but not a wife?"

My father gave a very clever answer as he quickly replied, "Go ask your mother." The humor in that illustration is often translated into many sad realities. Far too often the simple will ask questions of their parents or leaders and they will punt. When the questions of the simple are ignored or not answered properly by the Christian influences, the (wrong) answers will be found in the world. At that point the opportunity to direct the simple toward wisdom is lost and they will veer off toward foolishness.

The simple need answers to questions like, "Should a man marry a man or a woman marry a woman?" They are wondering, "How do I know if I'm a boy or a girl and can I decide for myself?" There are questions about the origins of the universe that sound like, "How did I get here and why am I here?" Confusion about the value of life leads to the question, "When does life begin?' They will even wonder, "How do I know I can trust the Bible?" There is no age limit for providing answers to these questions. Parents and Christian leaders need to be ready to give an answer to their questions (1 Peter 3:5).

Paul's admonishment in 2 Timothy 4:2 to be instant in season and to view each moment as a potential discipleship moment is so relevant to the leading of the simple toward wisdom. When Christian leaders are asked a question they need to provide a biblical answer. If they don't know the answer they need to find it. Punting and ignoring questions are not options. Talking down to the simple only keeps them down. Instead, talk up to them—which will cause them to grow in their respect for authority and develop a desire to travel on the journey toward wisdom.

PRESERVING THE SIMPLE
Without a doubt, the greatest need of the simple is to learn the Word of God. The Word of God is constantly being attacked and undermined on a variety of fronts. There are some vital areas that Christian leaders (parents in

70

particular) should address. The local church can play an important role in leading the simple toward wisdom.

When the Body of Christ is dwelling together in unity and the gifts of the Spirit are in operation, the members become stronger and more mature (Ephesians 4:11-13; Romans 12:4-8; 1 Corinthians 12:1-11). The simple need this strength and maturity displayed before them as an example. "Not forsaking the assembling of ourselves together, as the manner of some is; but exhorting one another: and so much the more, as ye see the day approaching" (Hebrew 10:25).

As I stated earlier, I started attending church nine months before I was even born. My parents took our family to Sunday school, Sunday morning and evening services, mid-week services and any special services that might have arisen. We were what was considered regular "churchgoers." I've been around long enough to see a change in what is considered "regular church attendance." While three times a week was once considered regular, it now seems that for many, the occasional Sunday morning is all it takes to be "regular" church attendees.

A 2016 Gallop Poll discovered that 40 percent of Americans, when asked, claimed to have attended a church service within a seven day period. This poll also clarified that only 26 percent of all Americans attend church weekly while 48 percent report only attending "seldom" or "never." The Barna Group has concluded that less than a third (31 percent) of Americans actually practice their faith. Attending church at least once per month is a primary indicator of whether someone actually practices their faith.

There is no biblical formula for the number of times in a given week or month that a believer should attend a church service. However, Hebrews 10:25 indicates that as we observe the world around us and are constantly reminded of the soon return of the Lord, the trend for gathering together with other believers should be on the increase. Yet just the opposite is occurring. We are on a downward trend in church attendance and the victims of this trend are the simple.

I have addressed the importance of how the Church must prioritize ministering to the simple. Parents also need to make church attendance a priority for their children. This is true particularly of fathers. Research conducted in Switzerland in 1994 and published in 2000 indicated that if both parents were regular churchgoers about 33 percent of their children would also become regular church attendees.

If the father was irregular or did not participate in church attendance at all then there was only a 2-3 percent chance that the children would become regular church attendees. This was true regardless of the attendance habits of the mother. However, if the father did attend church regularly but the mother was irregular or did not participate at all then the children were 38-44 percent likely to become regular church attendees.

The overall conclusion of the study was that if the father did not regularly attend church then there was only a 1 in 50 chance that his child would ever attend church. Fathers that did attend church regularly resulted in between two-thirds and three-fourths of their children becoming churchgoers (regularly or irregularly).

Take a look around at your next church service, and you will see that the trend in the world is that there is a gender gap. Women outnumber men in church services all around the world. Pew Research indicates this to be true globally, but it is quite pronounced in the United States. The gap between women and men attending religious services has been as high as 13 percentage points in favor of women over the last thirty years.

The 2016 statistics show that the gap has narrowed down to 6 percent, with the caveat that many women have stopped attending services altogether. Young people desperately need the example of both parents faithfully attending church together to serve as a positive example for their children to follow.

A key factor in the simple becoming wise is that they become lifelong church attendees. However, the chances of this happening are greatly diminished if the parents do not take on an active leadership responsibility to that end.

EDUCATION
"Beware lest any man spoil you through philosophy and vain deceit, after the tradition of men, after the rudiments of the world, and not after Christ" (Colossians 2:8). I am fortunate to be part of a unique brand of evangelicals. In my lifetime I never once attended a public school. My parents were committed to providing me and my sisters with a Christian education and as a result, we only attended Christian schools operated by evangelical churches.

My wife and I are also convinced of the necessity of providing our children with a Christian education and will not send them to a secular school. If one of our children were to be placed in a room with fifteen other children from homes of evangelical leaders, he or she would likely be the only child in the classroom that never attended a public school. An August 2012 survey conducted by the National Association of Evangelicals revealed that 93 percent of evangelical leaders have sent their children to public schools for part or all of their education. A majority (51 percent) have used public schools exclusively.

Let's be real; public schools are in a deplorable state and a direct reflection of the culture. They have become breeding grounds for political and social transformation for the secular left. There are few more hostile environments toward Christianity than the public schools where prayer and the Bible were declared unconstitutional by the Supreme Court of the United States. Without a doubt, there are many great teachers, but they are trapped in a system that prohibits them from openly sharing the truth of God's Word. The Scriptures are deliberately being undermined by the public education system.

In 1984 I was ready to enter kindergarten and my parents had to make a decision about where to send me to school. This was the first time they were faced with a schooling decision for their children. They had taken me to the local public school for a day to see how things were done. To this day I remember sitting down for story time and a teacher reading a picture book about dinosaurs and ape-like men. My little four-year-old brain was racing as I realized they were talking about evolution and even though I didn't completely understand the concept, I knew my parents had told me it was wrong and God had created the earth.

After that very brief encounter with the public school system, my parents made the decision to send me to a Christian school instead. The teaching I was receiving at home would be reinforced at that school and not undermined. They were concerned with what they saw in the public schools and wanted to guard me against any false teachings. This was a full twenty years before gay marriage was legalized and now taught in public schools as a viable "marriage" alternative to true biblical marriage. And over thirty years before transgender bathroom rights in public schools were even on anyone's radar.

The apostle Paul gave a very strong warning against allowing humanistic philosophies and secular worldviews to spoil the believer. Yet that is exactly what public education is doing to so many simple ones. But I wholeheartedly acknowledge that there are many young people that have gone through the public education system and have survived. But no one can deny that much of the education those students received was contrary to a biblical worldview.

One hour of church per week (or month in many cases) cannot counter thirty plus hours of secular education. The simple are shaping their view of the world. The education they receive will be a catalyst toward the direction which they will go—toward wisdom or folly.

The words "educate" or "education" do not appear in the Scriptures. Countless admonitions to "teach" and the core concept of educating certainly can be found throughout the Bible. The New Testament term that stands in for "education" is "discipleship."

The Great Commission as stated in Matthew 28:19 is clear about the necessity of discipleship. "Therefore, go and make disciples of all the nations, baptizing them in the name of the Father and the Son and the Holy Spirit" (New Living Translation). The King James Version uses "teach" in place of "make disciples."

Since education is actually discipleship it would seem obvious that a comparison of secular public education with Christian schools or Christian homeschooling programs would lead to a logical conclusion as to which is better for the child. Apparently, while the conclusion may be easy to reach, the practice is another matter as the majority of evangelical kids have never had any kind of Bible-based educational program. For many parents, it becomes an economic issue.

Public education is free, but a private Christian school or even homeschooling will have a cost associated with it. I would postulate that the cost is minor compared to the benefit of guarding the simple ones and guiding them to a worldview that is based in the fear of the Lord which propels them toward wisdom.

My wife and I are committed to Christian education for our children. We have invested tens of thousands of dollars and worked many extra jobs to make it possible because it is worth it. We have often said that we would sell our home and live in a ditch before we allowed our children to receive an education that was devoid of Christ.

A Turning Point

The path of the simple always leads to a turning point—a fork in the road with the option of turning toward folly or wisdom. Proverbs chapter nine describes a contrast between Lady Wisdom and Dame Folly. They call out to those passing by calling them to come into their houses. Verse four, wisdom's call, and verse sixteen, folly's lure give an identical illustration:

> "Whoso is simple, let him turn in hither: and as for him that wanteth understanding, she saith to him…"

The simple are being courted by both wisdom and folly. Youth is the crucial staging ground of the journey. So many would like to rush through that stage or cannot wait for it to be over. Yet God has planned it as a time in our lives when godly leadership can cultivate the simple in the fear of the Lord. It is during that time and much earlier as young children—that the simple must be pointed toward wisdom's cry.

Points to Ponder

- Do I recognize how important the simple are to the Lord?
- Does my church prioritize ministering to the simple?
- Am I prepared to give answers to the questions that youth ask? Do I at least know where to find the answers?
- What is my commitment to church attendance and discipleship like?

Chapter Ten

⚓

Do Not Enter

WITHOUT A DOUBT, the wildest traveling adventure I have ever experienced was while visiting New York City with some family members. I have driven on the bumpiest of back roads that don't even deserve to be called roads—they should simply be called giant potholes or ruts. But I have never taken part in anything as mind-boggling as trying to drive my car through the heavily congested streets of Manhattan on a Sunday afternoon. Cars and people were everywhere. Impatient taxi drivers didn't always wait in traffic. Some of them just jumped the curb and drove their vehicles on sidewalks to get past some traffic jams. It was a totally wild experience!

My family was divided into two cars. I was the follower and it was obvious we didn't have a clue as to how to get where we were going. We began to take some turns here and there and ended up taking a left turn at one point heading downhill into what looked like a tunnel. The tunnel, however, was actually a bus terminal and we were heading the wrong way down a one way road! There we were, two cars headed directly into an oncoming city bus, and it was not slowing down for anything. That bus came charging out of the tunnel, horn blowing, as we raced to do a three-point turn and reversed our direction. Since I was the follower, it was my car that almost kissed the bumper of the bus.

As the simple mature, they will be faced with directional decisions. Will they go down the one-way street of wisdom or will they dare to ignore the "Do Not Enter" signs that warn against going in the direction of foolishness? There are two people that can be found in the direction of foolishness—the scorner and the fool. Both need to be understood not only for identification but also for the sake of reformation and redirection toward wisdom.

THE SCORNER

Many years ago I had a student, a young lady, who had a particular habit that became very apparent after only a very short time. Every time she spoke of her mother, when she quoted something she had said—or spoke of something her mother had told her to do, she would turn up one side of her mouth so that her eye and cheek were twisted.

This student would also distort her voice into a very high-pitched mocking sound as if that was what her mother actually sounded like. She would be talking to her friends during recess or lunch and say something like, "So my mom said, 'Go clean your room.'" Without exception, she would always twist her face and change her voice during the quote. I soon began to realize that what she was doing was being scornful.

The scorner is mentioned thirteen times in the book of Proverbs. The word is derived from the Hebrew word *luwts* meaning to make mouths at, i.e. to scoff (Strong's Concordance n.d.). Webster's dictionary defines the scorner as "one who holds something in contempt or disdain." Repeatedly, the scorner is described in Proverbs as one who disregards the counsel and instruction of authority. He is described as one who hates his parents/teachers and essentially plugs his ears to keep from hearing their instruction (Proverbs 9:8; 13:1). He views their ways and what they have to say as repulsive and intrusive; he acts contemptibly toward them.

Many teenagers struggle with being scornful. Around the time that they are beginning to exert independence they frequently struggle with their response to what they view as an intrusion by authority. Often their mantra becomes, "It's my life, I can do what I want with it." Or, "I'm an adult now. You can't tell me what to do!" These scornful rebellious phrases are commonly uttered by teens and young adults. Often their attitude of independence is accompanied with a look of disdain—the rolling of the eyes, the shaking of the head and a contemptuous smile.

Rejection of the role of authority is the greatest risk factor for the scorner. Because of the role that parents and authority figures play in a successful journey toward wisdom, scorners are at a great disadvantage. The scorner has no ability to grasp wisdom because he has a complete disdain for his parents. The scorner refuses to receive instruction from anyone and has contempt for the corrector. Rejection of the necessary leadership needed to journey toward wisdom results in wide-ranging problems for scorners, making them especially vulnerable to the traps of the wicked.

> "Reprove not a scorner lest he hate thee" (Proverbs 9:8).

> "A wise son heareth his father's instruction: but a scorner heareth not rebuke" (Proverbs 13:1).

The scornful often have an attraction to wicked and ungodly people. It always amazes me that in groups of hundreds or even thousands of young people, the scorners can sniff each other out. Like a homing pigeon finding its way home, scorners can just somehow find each other. I am not the first to make this observation, but I can confirm that it is very true. It always seems that the kids with bad attitudes quickly discover one another, hang out together and feed off of each other.

Psalm 1 gives some glaring insights into the life of a scornful person, illustrating that he *chooses* to associate with ungodly, unrepentant sinners because that is where he is comfortable and wants to be.

Perhaps the most identifying characteristic of a scorner is his "I don't care" attitude and negative outlook on life in general. Scorners have no motivation to accomplish even simple tasks. A scorner is his own boss accomplishing tasks when "in the mood" or when he "feels like it." Scorners are lazy people.

The book of Proverbs is filled with messages about lazy individuals. There are two types of lazy people. The first type of lazy person is translated as sluggard or slothful from the Hebrew word *remîyâh* and refers to the one who does work, but does a sloppy job with an attitude of indifference. "The slothful man roasteth not that which he took in hunting" (Proverbs 12:27). The work that he does often needs to be redone and requires close supervision by those who are diligent.

Proverbs 12:24 implicitly states, "The hand of the diligent shall bear rule: but the slothful shall be under tribute." The scorner will always be *remîyâh* (unmotivated, lazy) because it is indigenous to his character. He will not live up to his full-potential because he lacks the motivation to apply himself to tasks.

The second kind of lazy person in Proverbs comes from the Hebrew word *atsel* and is the one who does not work. He always has an excuse for not working, sleeps a lot and is described in Proverbs as so lazy that he won't even take his hand out of his pocket to feed himself (Proverbs 26:13-15).

Slothfulness and sluggishness are two significant characteristics of a scorner. Scorners make for difficult students and terrible employees. It is interesting to note that Psalm 1:1 gives a warning against sitting in the seat of the scornful. The scorner is lazy because he has no higher purpose than satisfying his own whims and desires. What a miserable life to lead! If only the scorner would come to the realization that there is a higher purpose for which to live. If he could see that wisdom is of the utmost importance, he would abandon his scornful attitude and the harmful behavior that comes with it.

The book of Proverbs gives some carefully crafted instructions on how to properly deal with a scorner. While the simple require structure and accountability, the scorner requires harshness and isolation. The simple are very impressionable and are attracted to scorners. All too often the scorner is seen as the "cool kid" or someone who exerts leadership in a group. This attracts the simple to the scorner to his own detriment. Because of this, authorities are commanded to deal harshly with the scorner to deter the simple from following his example. "Smite the scorner and the simple will beware" (Proverbs 19:25).

The primary purpose of harsh correction is not to change the scorner; it will not. The purpose is symbolic—aimed toward the simple. Discipline toward the scorner is to be carried out as an example to the simple—as to what will happen if he follows in the scorner's footsteps. In addition to harsh treatment as a warning to the simple, all association and communication with the scorner must completely stop. It seems that contention follows scorners wherever they go. The problems arise because the scorner is unteachable, lazy and despises all authority. Scorners are often fired from jobs, suspended from school or barred from many different types of events. "Cast out the scorner, and contention shall go out; yea, strife and reproach shall cease" (Proverbs 22:10).

In Psalm 1:1 a blessing is given to those who do not sit in the seat of the scornful. It seems scorners have a talent for dragging others into scorning with them and should be avoided. In my experience as an educator, I have seen countless times the effect that a change in environment can have on the performance of a student. Again and again over the years I have seen students who were struggling socially, academically and behaviorally—turn-around completely when taken out of an environment that was influencing them negatively. By placing them into the safer environment of a good Christian school or homeschool, these troubled students were able to blossom and grow.

The company a person keeps has an effect, good or bad. Paul's admonition to the Corinthian church still holds true, "Don't be fooled by those who say such things, for bad company corrupts good character" (1 Corinthians 15:33, New Living Translation). All too often the pattern occurs of first hanging out with the scorner, followed by acting like a scorner, resulting in becoming a scorner. Stay away from scorners and keep your children away from them as well!

THE FOOL

In Matthew 5:22 Jesus is cited as speaking about three levels of anger that place people in danger of personal judgment:

1. Those who are angry without a cause.

2. Those who allow their anger to escalate to the point that they hurl the insult, "racca" (a Hebrew term meaning "empty-headed" whose modern-day equivalent would resemble "idiot"). Those who hurled this insult were in danger of the Sanhedrin council which was a more severe court than the simple level of judgment.

3. Those who elevated their insults to the level of calling someone a "fool" were in danger of hell fire.

In the Scriptures there is no greater insult than to be called a fool. In the Jewish mindset, the most deplorable of people who were wicked and completely immoral were categorized as fools. When a person can be identified as a scorner, he or she is in a position that is not favorable in light of Scripture. Anyone regarded as a fool is considered much worse. English translations of the book of Proverbs present three different Hebrew words for "fool." The first is *eviyl* (19 times), the second is *keciyl* (41 times), and the third is *nabal* (2 times).

Each of these terms are used in commonality to describe individuals who have rejected instruction and have elevated themselves to such an extent that their own self-confidence prohibits them from placing their trust in God. The lack of understanding of God's ways results in an embrace of immorality and a deluge of negative characteristics and painful consequences.

The most common characteristic of fools is their rejection of instruction (Proverbs 1:22; 15:5). The fool hates to learn from others. It is this rejection that results in many avoidable negative circumstances. Rather than garner wisdom from those who have gone before him, the fool insists on living defiantly and self-righteously.

PRACTICAL ATHEISM

The fool's greatest problem is his heart condition. Psalm 14:1 and 53:1 both make the same commentary concerning the fool (*nabal*) – "The fool has said in his heart, *There is* no God." The key to understanding this verse is the phrase "in his heart." It is not that the fool has necessarily defamed the existence of God with his mouth, but that he has rejected God's authority over him internally. Matthew Henry states it well in his commentary on Psalm 53:1:

> They cannot doubt of the being of God, but will question His dominion. He says this in his heart; it is not his judgment, but his imagination. He cannot satisfy himself that there is none, but he wishes there were none, and pleases himself with the fancy that is it possible there may be none. He cannot be sure there is one, and therefore he is willing to think there is none. He dares not speak it out, lest he be confuted, and so undeceived, but he whispers it secretly in his heart, for the silencing of the clamours of his conscience and the emboldening **of** himself in his evil ways.

Charles Spurgeon, in his book *Treasury of David*, refers to this as "practical atheism." This type of atheism is not theoretically opposed to God, but for all practical purposes—denies the existence of God through lifestyle. Chapters 14 and 53 in the book of Psalms describe the extreme wickedness of these fools.

No wonder the wise man's ongoing plea is, "Keep thy heart with all diligence; for out of it are the issues of life" (Proverbs 4:23). The fool's hope is that he will respond to the call of wisdom: "My son, give me thine heart, and let thine eyes observe my ways" (Proverbs 23:26). Two causes of folly are very common: The first is the conscious rejection of wisdom. Simply put, the fool hates knowledge (Proverbs 1:20-29; 10:23; 13:19; 29:27). Wisdom is too high a goal for the fool (Proverbs 24:7). He cannot attain it because he does not have the right heart condition to pursue it, and will not follow directions toward it.

The second cause of foolishness is when a person follows his heart (Proverbs 28:26). Because he rejects wisdom he turns to his own heart for counsel. But Scripture warns us that "The heart *is* deceitful above all *things*, and desperately wicked: who can know it?" (Jeremiah 17:9).

The majority of secular media and pop culture council the individual to "follow your heart." This is a fool's advice! The heart cannot be trusted to make wise choices and the Scriptures always advise believers to be led by the Holy Spirit, not the flesh/heart. Yet, the fool is continually finding and causing trouble because he follows his heart.

THERE IS NO GOD

Let's return to the problem of godlessness for the fool. The fool has clearly rejected the authority of God over his life, which is the primary root of his folly. The American culture at large is becoming more godless. The nation has experienced a rapid rise of agnosticism and atheism and this is indicative of the prevalence of foolishness.

The Pew Research Center conducted large-scale religious surveys in 2007 and 2014. These surveys revealed that within a seven-year period of time the percentage of those affiliated with the Christian faith decreased by 7.8 percent while those with no religious affiliation rose by 6.7 percent. During that time period, those claiming to be atheist and agnostic nearly doubled.

Estimates of the number of self-proclaimed atheists in the U.S.A. range from 3-11 percent. Some studies indicate that due to the social stigma of atheism the percentage may be as high as 26 percent with many "closet atheists" covering up their belief (or lack thereof). The obvious deduction from these statistics is that the current cultural trend is foolishness. There is certainly ample evidence to back up this assertion in the present culture.

Whether the number is 3 percent or 26 percent representing theoretical atheists, it is blatantly obvious that there is an abundance of practical atheists. While wisdom is the pursuit of God and based in the fear of the Lord, foolishness is exactly the opposite. The fool is running away from God and living a life that is void of the fear of God and replaces it with self-worship.

Many people will acknowledge the existence of God, but live in such a way as to deny His holy attributes. These are the fools of the world. In his commentary on Psalm 14:1, Charles Ryrie defined the fool as: "One who is morally perverse, not mentally deficient. [He] is described as to his belief, ('no God') and behavior ('no good'). His is a practical rather than a theoretical atheist."

In many ways it appears that the cohorts of the foolish have launched a full-scale attack on the ways of the wise. There is a tremendous attack on faith in the culture in general that goes beyond the silly attempts at banning the phrase "Merry Christmas" every December. The incessant drip of a perverse culture and the perpetual attempts to undermine the Scriptures are chipping away at the youth in our churches to the point that many are beginning to doubt fundamental doctrines.

When faith in God is undermined, the very foundation of wisdom is destroyed, preventing the ability to achieve it. The Church cannot allow the foolishness of this world to invade its sanctuaries. It must harden its resolve to defend against the wiles of the enemy. The Church must take on the full-armor of God and pursue wisdom while defending its foundations for the generations to come (Ephesians 6:11).

Points to Ponder

- Can I recognize scorners and avoid them as well as protect my friends and family from them?

- Have I fallen for the lies of the culture that say, "Follow your heart"?

- Is my heart secretly denying there is a God by the actions I take?

- Do I have a law of the home that ensures discipline will be administered to drive out foolishness and promote wisdom?

Chapter Eleven

$$\maltese$$

Strategies for Positive Growth

O N A WARM summer afternoon some years ago, I took my children to the local park to expend some energy. My wife and I have three boys and one girl. At that time their ages ranged from five to ten years old. The trip was to be short-lived. One of our boys decided that he did not want to follow my instructions. He wanted to do what he wanted to do and he became quite belligerent about it, resulting in the necessity of a quick retreat from the park and a dash home so his unacceptable behavior could be appropriately addressed.

DISCIPLINE
During the ride home as I was pondering my son's actions, the Holy Spirit impressed upon me that these actions were a reflection of the heart. Proverbs 22:15 reveals, "Foolishness is bound in the heart of a child; but the rod of correction shall drive it far from him." My son was exhibiting the foolishness bound in his heart. True, but the broader point was that it didn't have to stay that way. It could be driven out of him, and as his father I want nothing better for him than to reject the paths of fools and pursue the way of wisdom.

When we arrived at home I looked into his eyes and said, "Son, the way you acted was foolish and your mother and I are going to drive that foolishness out of you." The greatest opportunity for directing an individual away from foolishness and toward wisdom is during childhood. Often the period of adolescence is marked by scornful or foolish behavior. But childhood presents an opportunity to drive out foolishness from the heart.

The method for doing this is discipline (the rod of correction). Parents bear the brunt of this responsibility and it is one of the most loving things that a parent can do for his or her child. In his book, *Bringing Up Boys*, Dr. James Dobson references a quote that states, "Children need to learn that love can frown." It isn't always pleasant, but it is always necessary.

> "Now no chastening for the present seemeth to be joyous, but grievous: nevertheless afterward it yieldeth the peaceable fruit of righteousness unto them which are exercised thereby" (Hebrews 12:11).

Discipline is not something done "to" the child—but rather "for" the child. Dr. Dobson further states, "The word discipline connotes not only the shaping of a child's behavior and attitudes but also giving him a measure of self-control and the ability to delay gratification." In this way, discipline becomes a gift to the child that drives away foolishness and steers him toward wisdom.

Discipline is tough to administer. As a parent, I can still clearly remember the gut-wrenching feeling I had when I first disciplined my oldest child and she began to cry. The only thing that kept me from giving in to her tears was quoting Proverbs 19:18 to myself. "Chasten thy son [or daughter] while there is hope, and let not thy soul spare for his crying." I wanted to go easy and relieve the temporary pain that she was experiencing, but I needed to trust the Scriptures and realize that this was what was needed for her long-term good.

There must be consequences for scornful and foolish actions. Without consequences to match the severity of the offense the child will be emboldened to continue those actions. Solomon emphasizes this point in his philosophical ponderings of life in Ecclesiastes 8:11: "Because sentence against an evil work is not executed speedily, therefore the heart of the sons of men is fully set in them to do evil."

Foolishness is already in a child's heart. We are all born with the sin nature and have the propensity to think and behave foolishly. Without firm and loving direction from parents and other authority figures, along with strategic implementation of discipline, children will be foolish. They require molding through discipline; not only to drive out foolishness but also to be directed toward wisdom. "The rod and reproof give wisdom: but a child left to himself bringeth his mother to shame" (Proverbs 29:15).

Discipline is a two-edged sword that drives out foolishness. But more important, discipline cultivates wisdom. A full discussion of the necessity of discipline for driving out foolishness demands a discussion on methods of discipline. For many, this discussion has evolved into a debate: "To spank, or not to spank? That is the question." There is much debate as to whether or not spanking a child as a form of discipline is appropriate or helpful and the issue has become very polarizing.

Over recent years a growing opposition to physical punishment has been expressed in the medical and psychology fields. (Thankfully it has not yet penetrated Christian psychology completely.) That belief is fueled by controversial studies on the negative effects of physical punishment on children. The United Nations Committee on the Rights of the Child has proclaimed physical punishment as "legalized violence against children" and it seeks to eliminate it through any means available, including legal means. Many countries around the world have banned physical punishment because of this trend.

The overriding scriptural precedent is the necessity of discipline. The book of Proverbs promotes spanking as a primary tool (Proverbs 22:15; 23:13). The problem of child abuse is real and prevalent and where the administration of spanking runs afoul for so many. Nowhere in Scripture is the abuse of a child ever promoted. In fact, Jesus was very clear that those who were abusive to children were better off dead due to how serious the judgment upon their lives would be (Matthew18:6; Mark 9:42; Luke 17:1-2). When the biblical principle of discipline is practiced, positive physical punishment can produce the desired result of driving out foolishness and directing a child toward wisdom.

The important point to remember is this: How to discipline a child should not deteriorate into a debate about methodology. Whether spanking is implemented or not, the priority remains that foolishness must be driven out of a child. Nothing is more dangerous to children than the foolishness bound in their hearts. When authority figures refuse to implement discipline over children—foolishness prevails with little hope of a child ever growing toward and gaining wisdom.

Unfit for Office

Proverbs 26:1-12 is dedicated to the description of fools. Included with the very colorful descriptions are also some very vivid warnings about them. The fool and scorner are completely untrustworthy and are not fit to hold positions of leadership. Employers should not hire them or at the very least, not allow them to be in a leadership position. This is important and clearly warned against in the Scriptures.

Throughout my career as an educator it has been suggested that students who struggle with their attitudes and actions need some responsibility to help straighten them out. I have heard of scorners being assigned as tutors or assistants to other students, hoping the responsibility will help them behave more appropriately. It sounds very idealistic but it's not a biblical approach. It is not a realistic way to deal with scorners. "He that sendeth a message by the hand of a fool cutteth off *his own* feet, *and* drinketh in damage" (Proverbs 26:6, American Standard Version). Never give a scorner or fool influence. It won't turn out well.

Churches should view fools and scorners as opportunities for evangelism and strive to bring them the love of Christ. But under no circumstances should a fool be allowed to be in a position of leadership or influence. They should especially never be allowed to hold positions of influence in children's and youth ministries. Regardless of any talent or abilities, the scorner and the fool are unfit for office. Their influence will never be positive and anything that they might bring to the table will be completely underwhelmed by their negative characteristics.

Fools Refuse to Receive Instruction

The fool's biggest problem is that he or she refuses to receive instruction. The constant refrain in the book of Proverbs regarding fools is that they simply refuse to receive constructive guidance from anybody. No one can tell them anything.

During a conversation with a student who had graduated from the Christian school where I am the principal, the topic of other classmates came up. I have seen too many young people abandon the Church and faith after leaving high school. I asked the student why he thought this happened to some of his classmates. He explained to me that he believed it was because they had so many questions about the Bible which were not satisfactorily answered. This produced doubts and an eventual abandoning of the faith. He then mentioned a few of the questions that caused doubt.

I was very interested in hearing him out because I wanted to see what I could do to help improve this problem. But I knew that most, if not all of the questions that were being asked had actually been addressed in the curriculum of the school program; there were also specific apologetic classes that provided biblical answers to practical questions and relevant cultural issues.

The problem isn't always unanswered questions. Sometimes it's unreceived answers. That is not to imply that these young people didn't have legitimate questions that needed to be addressed. The Lord invites everyone to come and reason together with Him because He wants to give answers to questions and meet our greatest needs (Isaiah 1:18). But we must be willing to *receive* the instruction provided by those answers.

My father has been pastoring for over three decades. I have often heard a sad lament regarding his congregation. I have witnessed my parents offer hours of counseling to many church members who were struggling in marriage, with emotions, with children, etc. I have heard my father decry the fact that so much of the counseling he does wouldn't be necessary if people would just receive the instruction he gives in his sermons. Too often, the instruction that pastors give in church services to their congregations go in one ear and out the other. There is much wisdom in the scriptural instruction provided by pastors every week from the pulpit. If only the Church as a whole would receive the messages given instead of just listening to the sermons.

HOPE FOR THE FOOL

Statistically, there is hope for the world regarding fools. Apparently and thankfully, fools are not good at reproducing themselves. The Pew Research Center has projected that those unaffiliated with a religion (including atheists and agnostics) will *decrease* in percentage over the next several decades.

The fool's primary issue takes place in his heart where he denies God's place of authority in his life. When that issue is addressed, the fool can be gloriously reformed. What will this require? It requires going to the root of the problem First, repentance is necessary. Only when the fool sees the error of his ways and the insanity of his folly will he be motivated to acknowledge that he is wrong and God is right. This is a regenerative work of the Holy Spirit in the fool's life. It must be the Holy Spirit because the fool won't listen to anyone else. When this shift in attitude occurs the fool is postured for a change of heart.

When describing the results of repentance the prophet Ezekiel wrote in chapter 11 verse 19, "And I will give them one heart, and I will put a new spirit within you; and I will take the stony heart out of their flesh, and will give them an heart of flesh."

The fool needs a spiritual heart transplant because he does not have a heart for wisdom (Proverbs 17:16). This radical change is available to anyone who will repent and turn to the Lord. There is a difference between a fool and foolish acts. The battle with the sin nature will continue as long as we are on this earth, and there will be times when an individual commits a foolish act. That doesn't necessarily make him a fool any more than a moment of wisdom makes a person wise. Foolish acts most certainly must be recognized, but it is also necessary to be able to identify and evangelize a fool.

Steering away from the path of foolishness and traveling toward wisdom is what people need to do. This will only happen when self-confidence and self-reliance philosophies are abandoned in favor of the fear of the Lord, and accepting His divine instructions. It's time to get off the path of fools which leads to destruction and journey toward the way of wisdom and a fulfilling life.

Points to Ponder

- Am I willing to recognize authority and receive instruction?

- Is there foolishness in my heart that needs to be driven out?

- Do I have a law of the home that ensures discipline will be administered to drive out foolishness and promote wisdom?

- Am I praying for and evangelizing the scorners and fools?

Chapter Twelve

⚓

The Final Destination

WHILE A FRESHMAN in Bible college, I was offered the opportunity to take a trip to Hawaii with some friends. The parent of one of my friends was able to get tickets and accommodations for the entire trip, and it would only cost each of us a mere fifty dollars. I was only nineteen and it seemed like the chance of a lifetime. I was very tempted by the lure of the trip, and my parent's said that I could make the decision on my own without them trying to influence me. If I chose to go I would miss over a week of classes. I didn't want the trip to interfere with my academic studies, so I decided not to go. I told my friends that I didn't think it would be "prudent" for me to go at that time. I would loved to have taken the trip, but the better decision at that time was for me to focus on my studies. Prudence always chooses the *better* things.

THE PRUDENT

When the simple are at the crossroads of life they will lean either toward folly or wisdom. The first step on the path toward wisdom and away from folly is prudence. In Proverbs the words prudent and prudence, as translated in the King James Version are derived from five different Hebrew words (*biyn, aram, aruwm, sakal,* and *ormah*). They are synonyms that refer to cunningness and discernment in a practical application to life. Webster's dictionary defines prudence this way: "The ability to govern and discipline oneself by the use of reason; skills and good judgment in the use of resources; caution or circumspection as to the danger or risk."

Prudence is common sense in action. "Every prudent man dealeth with knowledge," according to Proverbs 13:16. A prudent person is able to make mature decisions that lead to positive outcomes. Young people who deny themselves the pleasure of late night activities before a big event demonstrate prudence (to ensure that they will do their best).

The average of over $15,000 in credit card debt per U.S. household is contrasted with the prudence of the young couple that scrimps and saves to make their major purchases. It doesn't take a genius to figure out the value of these things. It just takes some maturity through the application of common sense. "The simple inherit folly: but the prudent are crowned with knowledge" (Proverbs 14:18).

CHARACTERISTICS OF THE PRUDENT
The prudent are marked by a number of characteristics. They all revolve around the basic concept of mature decision-making in order to minimize negatives and maximize positives.

DISCERNMENT
The book of Proverbs describes the prudent as having an ability to examine the facts and discern the truth. They are contrasted with the simple who are gullible. "The simple believeth every word: but the prudent man looketh well to his going" (Proverbs 14:15). There are a lot of high-pressure sales tactics implemented in the modern economy. It is very easy to be taken in by a sweet-sounding deal or to simply just click the agree button without actually reading the fine print. Prudent people will not be easily taken in by slick strategies because they are "looking well to their going" and not falling for every offer or sales pitch that comes their way.

LIFELONG LEARNERS
The prudent are willing to be corrected when they are wrong so they can learn from their mistakes. Unlike the fool, the prudent are not interested in the school of hard knocks. If there is a better way to do things that will avoid problems they will choose that way. They are interested in efficiency and productivity and are willing to adapt and learn.

The term "lifelong learner" is a buzz-phrase in the world of leadership training. Professionals are expressing the importance and necessity of continued learning and growing for all those who hold leadership positions. This is an example of prudence. The prudent person isn't satisfied with stagnation, but wants growth and realizes that continuous learning from others is necessary. "A fool despiseth his father's instruction: but he that regardeth reproof is prudent" (Proverbs 15:5).

THINKING AHEAD

Perhaps the most predominant characteristic of the prudent is considering the consequences of decisions before taking action in any given circumstance. Prudence requires forethought and preparation. My wife and I have two sons with autism which brings with it many challenges. However, we have both learned how to "read" them and can often anticipate their response in a particular situation, and take steps to minimize or even eliminate their reactions. A prudent person looks ahead.

Prudence is like playing chess. A good chess player isn't just thinking about his next move. He's thinking about all the ramifications of his next move and carefully crafting it in such a way that opens up opportunities for the next several moves. He is thinking strategically. Prudence is strategic, which is one reason why it is a most desirable trait in leadership.

I can still remember the advice of my driving instructor during my driver's education course when I was fifteen. He said that we should be aware not only of the actions of the car directly in front of us, but also the other four or five cars in front that car. The actions of all those cars would eventually affect me and I would be a better driver by looking ahead and preparing for what may be coming.

Prudence built the insurance business. The reason for all the different kinds of insurance policies (health, auto, life, home, etc.) is to plan in advance and be prepared for future needs that may arise.

The weather in the Northeastern United States can be unpredictable, especially during the harsh winter months. It is not uncommon to lose several consecutive days of school due to blizzards or ice-storms. Paying very close attention to local weather reports is necessary. When I see the potential for some snow that might cause classes to be cancelled, I always encourage my students to be prudent and take some school work home.

A prudent person can look ahead and see when trouble might be approaching, and will abstain from the appearance of evil. Proverbs 22:3 and 27:12 both state, "A prudent man foreseeth the evil and hideth himself: but the simple pass on, and are punished." In commenting on this passage, Matthew Henry stresses the fact that, "Evil may be foreseen."

If a person is paying attention he can foresee what is ahead. The average young person knows that most unchaperoned high school or college parties will involve drinking, drugs, sex, etc. If he or she becomes involved in any of those things, it will not be an accidental involvement. The prudent person will anticipate the dangers of such parties and avoid them. Prudence is often just simply reading the situation and taking steps to avoid potential danger.

A prudent person is always looking ahead and planning in every area of his or her life. This includes the area of finances. Prudent people don't spend all their money; they carefully plan their budget and save. Savings are important because life is unpredictable. Insurance can cover specific things but there is always the potential for an emergency and prudent people will have an "emergency fund" of at least $1,000 to protect themselves.

> Prudence is like playing chess. A good chess player isn't just thinking about his next move.

A sad reality in the United States is that very little prudence is exercised in the area of savings. A 2017 nationwide survey found that more than half of all American adults (57 percent) admitted to having less than $1,000 in savings. Even more disturbing is the fact that 39 percent do not have any savings whatsoever, with some states reporting as high as 48 percent of resident adults having no savings. These people are living paycheck to paycheck and are one flat tire away from having to go into the bondage of debt. A prudent person takes precautions against any problems that might arise by having some savings.

When parents hire teenagers to babysit their children, they want them to be prudent so they can then count on them to be vigilant, observant and to think before acting. Prudent people are mature and exercise God-given faculties that enable them to make smart choices and avoid potential catastrophes—or at the very least be prepared for them.

Proverbs 19:14b states "...a prudent wife is from the Lord." I have been blessed with a very prudent wife. She manages our home with unmatched efficiency, constantly planning ahead for our family to ensure that every need is met. Clothes for the school week are prepared on weekends and neatly organized so that our children can get them with ease. Meals are planned and prepared in advance. She is a masterful shopper and is able to feed the entire household on a meager budget and still manage to stockpile reserves. The majority of our Christmas shopping is nearly always completed before Thanksgiving. She is a gift from God to me and her prudence is a tremendous blessing and value to our entire household.

DEVELOPING PRUDENCE

Prudence is a valuable virtue that should be developed in a person's life. The receipt of counsel and learning from the successes and failures of others can greatly assist in the development of prudence

RECEIVING COUNSEL WHEN NECESSARY

The central concept of prudence is circumspection. The prudent safeguard themselves and their loved ones by navigating cautiously through life. They are not necessarily afraid of risk, but they realize that unnecessary risk is just that—unnecessary. Prudence can be exhibited by actively pursuing the safety of trusted counsel when making major decisions. "Where no counsel is, the people fall: but in the multitude of counselors there is safety" (Proverbs 11:14). For example, a prudent person will obtain a vehicle history report and have a mechanic check out a car before agreeing to purchase it because he or she understands the value of good counsel.

Many pastors promote prudence by refraining from performing wedding ceremonies for couples that have not first received pre-marital counseling. Navigating the challenges of marriage within the first few years is overwhelming and newlyweds need all the sound counsel they can get. The decision to marry is so significant and important that prudence demands seeking the counsel of trusted advisers. This principal applies to many other areas of life. Significant decisions should be made with caution, while taking into consideration the advice of others who have "been there and done that."

THE PRUDENT FOLLOW THE POSITIVE EXAMPLES OF OTHERS

Receiving counsel as a means for developing prudence is linked to the second area—that of learning from the examples of others. There is much to be learned from others. This applies to both positive and negative behaviors. The mistakes others have made should serve as examples on how to avoid those same mistakes and their subsequent consequences. It is the fool who insists on having to figure it out on his or her own. The failures of others are a valuable learning tool and the prudent person will capitalize on those missteps.

This also applies in the realm of the positive. Emulating those who have experienced success is of tremendous value. Time, effort and pain can be avoided when good examples are followed. The apostle Paul urged the struggling Corinthian church to follow his instruction. They were failing miserably in many areas of their Christian walk. He encouraged them to follow his positive example as a successful believer. Paul himself was following the example of Christ (1 Corinthians 4:16; 11:1). Find successful individuals and learn from them. Attempt to identify and emulate those habits and traits that contribute to their success.

PRUDENCE IS **NOT** THE SAME AS WISDOM

Prudence is NOT wisdom. Proverbs 8:12 draws a connection between the two: "I wisdom dwell with prudence..." but prudence itself is not wisdom. While the wise will always display prudence, a display of prudence does not immediately confirm a person to be wise. The reason for this conclusion is that prudence is different than wisdom in its Source. Wisdom begins with a fear of the Lord and springs from God Almighty. Apart from a personal relationship with Jesus Christ, wisdom is unattainable.

The unsaved can be prudent by using their God-given abilities. Many successful people have gained much knowledge and understanding about worldly living, but they have not come to a saving knowledge of Jesus Christ. They may be some of the most heathen-like people and yet still exhibit prudence. Just because they are not saved does not mean that they cannot demonstrate prudence and offer sound, practical advice in many areas. Even Christ made the observation in Luke 16:8 that sometimes the prudence of the heathen is greater than the prudence of the saved. "And the Lord commended the unrighteous steward that he did prudently, because the sons of this age are more prudent than the sons of the light, in respect to their generation" (Young's Literal Translation).

While prudence is very beneficial it does not rise to the level of wisdom because it can be sourced from Man. Wisdom is far superior and should be pursued. Prudence can never equate to wisdom, for wisdom comes from a Source that is unequaled and unrivaled in every aspect.

The Wise

Wisdom is understood as a state of being in that it is truly living life the way that God intended. The wise, therefore, are those who are demonstrating wisdom. They are elevated in the Scriptures as those who have the best lives and the most blessings because that which makes them wise does not come from within them but rather wisdom's Source—God Almighty. The foundation for wisdom within the individual is rooted in the fear of the Lord.

Throughout history there have been many wise people. But there is only One who stands apart from the rest in the manifestation of wisdom in the totality of life. The Lord Jesus Christ is the ultimate example of a wise life. Every aspect of His life, His characteristics and His behaviors are the embodiment of the wise man. His life on this earth was a perfect reflection of the Father. All the things that Jesus did and said were not of Himself but were of the Father (John 8:28-29). He lived His life without sin in perfect harmony with the will of God the Father. He was uncorrupted by humanism and pride and only walked in the ways of wisdom. His very life was a spoken message from God the Father according to Hebrews 1:1-3:

> "God, who at sundry times and in divers manners spake in time past unto the fathers by the prophets, Hath in these last days spoken unto us by his Son, whom he hath appointed heir of all things, by whom also he made the worlds; Who being the brightness of his glory, and the express image of his person, and upholding all things by the word of his power, when he had by himself purged our sins, sat down on the right hand of the Majesty on high."

The life of Christ speaks to us affirming wisdom. The wise man must start his journey with a personal relationship with Christ. There is no mechanism for achieving wisdom apart from this. The ways of wisdom are the ways of God. The wise man as revealed in Proverbs responds to life in the grandest fashion possible. This is because the wise man responds to life as Jesus would.

Characteristics of the Wise

The characteristics of the wise are numerous. The book of Proverbs gives many detailed descriptions of the behavior of the wise in many facets of life. A predominant characteristic is willingness to receive and accept instruction. Over and over the refrain of the wise father in Proverbs is the reminder to his son to receive instruction:

- "To receive the instruction of wisdom…" (Proverbs 1:3).
- "My son if thou wilt receive my words, and hide my commandments with thee" (Proverbs 2:1).
- "My son, forget not my law; but let thine heart keep my commandments" (Proverbs 3:1).
- "Hear, ye children, the instruction of a father, and attend to know understanding" (Proverbs 4:1).
- "My son, attend to my words; incline thine ear unto my sayings" (Proverbs 4:20).
- "My son, attend unto my wisdom, and bow thine ear to my understanding" (Proverbs 5:1).
- "My son, keep my words, and lay up my commandments with thee. Keep my commandments, and live; and my law as the apple of thine eye" (Proverbs 7:1).

Similar, profound statements continue throughout the entire book of Proverbs. Receiving instruction is key to the development of the wise, making them polar opposites of the fool. Instruction is received with great humility, and faith is expressed by carrying through with the given directives.

Receiving instruction requires humility. Wisdom will exalt a life and the biblical formula is always to first: "Humble yourselves in the sight of the Lord, and he shall lift you up" (James 4:10). Receiving instruction requires an individual to put aside pride when thinking that his or her own way is best. This is not an easy task. The pride of life is quick to arise; the mortification of the deeds of the flesh can hurt and are not easily put to rest. Yet it is the humility to receive instruction that allows instruction to grow into a bountiful harvest. Humility is the key to unlocking the doors of wisdom.

> "Therefore, brethren, we are debtors, not to the flesh, to live after the flesh. For if ye live after the flesh, ye shall die: but if ye through the Spirit do mortify the deeds of the body, ye shall live" (Romans 8:12-13).

Another important element to receiving instruction is submission to authority. Over and over the father/son relationship is expressed in the book of Proverbs. It is understood that the only way for the son to be wise is to submit to the authority of his parents. Submission to authority is a powerful biblical principle that is all too often ignored. Its power is derived from the fact that authority is established by God. When we resist that authority we are in essence resisting God. When we submit to it, we are submitting to God (Romans 13). Rebellion, as the antithesis of submission is so far removed from God that it is equated to witchcraft, and the stubborn refusal to submit to authority is compared to idolatry (1 Samuel 15:23).

Submission to authority requires great faith. That faith was exemplified in the life of the Roman centurion as we can see in these verses:

> "And when Jesus was entered into Capernaum, there came unto him a centurion, beseeching him, and saying, Lord, my servant lieth at home sick of the palsy, grievously tormented. And Jesus saith unto him, I will come and heal him. The centurion answered and said, Lord, I am not worthy that thou shouldest come under my roof: but speak the word only, and my servant shall be healed. For I am a man under authority, having soldiers under me: and I say to this man, Go, and he goeth; and to another, Come, and he cometh; and to my servant, Do this, and he doeth it" (Matthew 8:5-9).

The centurion acknowledged to Jesus that he understood the structure of authority and how it functions. Jesus marveled at this man's faith, commenting that he had "not found so great faith, no, not in Israel" and the servant was healed (Matthew 8:10, 13).

Submitting to the instruction of others requires faith that God knows what He's doing in establishing authority. Too many young people fail to see the value of the role of the authority of parents, pastors, teachers and others—which God has gifted into their lives. The instruction that can be received from these authority figures can give wisdom when it is received in faith.

Several years ago our church started the new year off with a two-part series on handling finances God's way. I preached the series and it was both philosophical in regard to how money should be viewed, but also practical including steps for establishing a budget, paying off debt, etc. It has been my experience that many messages preached from the pulpit bear little fruit in the lives of the congregation (because of the propensity for the words to go in one ear and out the other). This seems particularly true of money. Nobody wants to be told what they should do with *their* money. However, one dear lady had not only heard the sermons but had also received some of the messages. I can remember her coming to me and thanking me for the teachings and telling me that she was going to try to get out of debt.

I didn't think too much of it at the time due to my skepticism about instruction actually being received. To my surprise, she came back to me several months later. She told me that she had been incorporating what I taught into the way she handles her finances, and that she was close to having her credit cards paid off.

Throughout the following months this determined lady continued to give me updates on how the Lord was providing for her. Someone even gave her a truck, so she was able to sell her car and pay off her car loan. She was not spending beyond her fixed income budget and was following the precepts I had taught in the financial sermon series. This wise lady was finding financial success and prosperity. About a year and a half after her journey to financial freedom began, she reported that she was debt free and God was blessing her household.

This wise lady then took it to another level and started giving. Frequently she would approach me or my wife after a service and shake our hands. In her hand would be some money that she would slip into one of our hands. She would have a big smile on her face as she did this. Whenever we would question her generosity she would always say that it was because I had taught her how God wanted her to use her money. Her future changed from a senior citizen in debt to a giver. She received instruction and it made her wise.

It is very rare for a person to receive *and* implement instruction. Far too often I have experienced the frustration of receiving training in a group setting only to find that the lectures were heard, but never implemented by all the participants. The wise man will not only be a hearer but a doer:

> "For if any be a hearer of the word, and not a doer, he is like unto a man beholding his natural face in a glass: For he beholdeth himself, and goeth his way, and straightway forgetteth what manner of man he was. But whoso looketh into the perfect law of liberty, and continueth therein, he being not a forgetful hearer, but a doer of the work, this man shall be blessed in his deed" (James 1:23-25).

WILLING TO RECEIVE CORRECTION

Related to the ability of the wise to receive instruction is the ability to also receive *correction*. The receipt of correction provides guidance. The ability to receive correction is essential in order to prevent tragedy and provide a reversal in course, when necessary. The wise will recognize and understand that correction serves as a warning sign of possible trouble ahead.

The importance of discipline has been addressed in detail because of its fundamental role in driving foolishness out of the heart. Discipline functions as a two-edged sword in not only driving out foolishness but also in giving wisdom. "The rod and reproof give wisdom: but a child left to himself bringeth his mother to shame" (Proverbs 29:15).

What sets the discipline of giving wisdom apart from discipline that drives out foolishness? It is the *way* in which it is received. A wise person will receive correction willingly and see the purpose behind it. This perspective enables him to see the love behind it and in turn produce a love for the one giving the correction. "Reprove not a scorner, lest he hate thee: rebuke a wise man, and he will love thee" (Proverbs 9:8).

Since the ultimate objective of the wise man is to live life as God intended, he willingly, even gladly, receives correction. He wants to avoid going the wrong way and therefore clearly sees the place and value of correction. The wise want to be told when they are in error so that they can immediately stop and adjust the course that they must take. Correction is highly valued by the wise and they willingly receive it.

KEEPING THINGS IN THEIR PROPER PERSPECTIVE

On an October day my family and I were out shopping. We came across a bin of merchandise in one of the store aisles and my youngest son, age five at the time, said, "Ew Halloween!" I looked down at him and all I could see was a bin full of cotton balls. I replied back to him, "That's not Halloween. It's a bunch of cotton balls." Then I looked lower at what he saw at his eye level and could see a bunch of Halloween pictures of ghosts and goblins. From his perspective he was right. He was seeing "yucky" pictures. But at my height I had a different perspective, only seeing fluffy cotton balls.

A distinguishing trait of the wise is their higher perspective. While the prudent are always looking ahead, the wise go beyond forward looking to being eternally minded. They understand that the value of their own lives and the lives of those around them—extend beyond the temporal into the eternal.

With this understanding comes a set of values that recognizes what will last and what is fleeting.

The missionary, Jim Elliot, is a hero of the faith. He was an extremely talented man with much potential. He surrendered his life to missions. He, along with four other wise men attempted to bring the gospel to the notorious Huaorani (or Auca) tribe of Ecuador. Their attempts were met with a violent response and all five of the men were martyred. The story of their sacrifice and devotion spread throughout the world and to many, it would seem that a life with so much potential was not only cut short, but wasted. However, Jim Elliot and his friends had a very different perspective. He once wrote, "He is no fool who gives what he cannot keep to gain what he cannot lose."

Jim Elliot realized that eternity matters much more than this temporal life. His concern and expenditures for the lost souls that he so desperately wanted to win for Christ were not wasted. His sacrifice was a temporary loss for an eternal gain. His wife and family members of the other brave martyrs continued that effort. These brave individuals went and preached to the murderers of their husbands and brothers and won them over for Jesus and even baptized them. By maintaining an eternal perspective, those missionaries demonstrated that they were wise. "The fruit of the righteous is a tree of life; and he that winneth souls is wise" (Proverbs 11:30).

The perspective of the wise not only extends beyond the temporal into eternity but also beyond the veil of the physical into the realm of the spiritual. In Ephesians 6:10-20, the apostle Paul vividly describes the unseen demonic forces in the world that are at work all around us. They must be resisted and opposed by utilizing the whole armor of God. A glimpse into the unseen realm makes us aware that there is much more to this life than that which can be seen. The wise understand this and can discern the hand of God at work all around them. They see not only with the physical eye but with the eye of faith. This is a lens that empowers and enables them to have the right perspective. Because they can see the hand of God at work, they will inherit honor and glory. "The wise shall inherit glory: but shame shall be the promotion of fools" (Proverbs 3:35).

I've been a Christian educator for over two decades. I've been privileged to observe the lives of my students not only during the grade school years but also to watch them grow into adults and begin careers. I've even had children of former students in my school. Over the years I've graduated many students and many of them are certainly prudent. They have gone on to enjoy success in college, career and family avoiding many of the pitfalls of life. I know their parents are proud of them and I also take pride in seeing young people go out and become successful in life knowing that I had a part in their life training.

I am so very proud of the extremely rare wise student who has passed through the halls of my school. It's a different kind of pride, though, because I didn't have much to do with those exceptional students attaining wisdom. I might have had a small part in leading them, but their wisdom came directly from God. I can't teach others to be wise, but I can point them to the Source of wisdom. There are no courses to take that issue certificates or diplomas in wisdom. The only way to get wisdom is to go directly to God Himself.

The exemplary students I have met were not satisfied with "good enough." They wanted God's best for their lives. That is what I want for every one of my students. It is the yearning of my father's heart for my children. It is also the deep desire of a pastor when he prays for his congregation—that somehow the cry of wisdom will be heard—even in the midst of all of life's daily distractions, then pursued with passion.

To become one of the wise should be the highest priority in life. The final destination on life's journey is to be one of those rare individuals who can truly claim the title: A Wise Person.

POINTS TO PONDER

- Do I understand prudence and can I demonstrate it?
- Does my leadership style reflect prudence?
- Am I consciously developing prudence in my life through a willingness to receive counsel and seek it out as well as emulating positive role models?
- Am I putting forth the effort necessary to receive instruction?
- Even if I initially bristle at it, do I come around to receiving correction even from those close to me—like my spouse, parents, co-workers, etc.?
- Is my perspective focused on the eternal with an understanding of the invisible spiritual forces at work all around me?

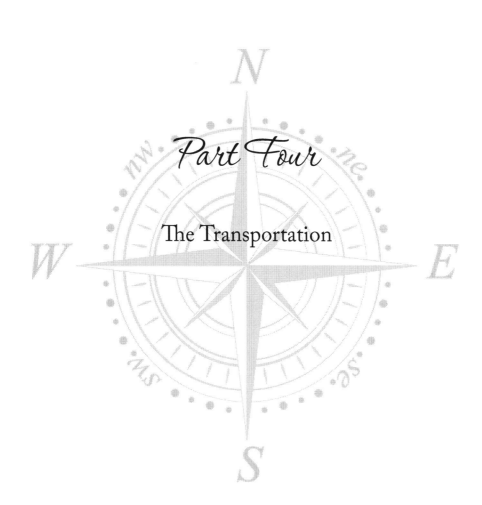

Part Four

The Transportation

Chapter Thirteen

⚓

Purity First

But the wisdom that is from above is first pure...
James 3:17

I ENJOY TRAVELING AND ministering to people. The majority of my life's work has been serving people throughout the United States. I have had the opportunity to reach out to the rugged individualists of the Northwest, the blue-collar workers of the heartland and the hospitable southerners of the Bible Belt. My trips have always been enjoyable and unencumbered. But that changed when I had the opportunity to minister in Asia. The entire trip became a bit more complicated. I had been dragging my feet on completing my passport application. I knew I needed one, but I wasn't fully aware of exactly how important it was until it came time to secure the airline tickets.

I have never had any trouble getting a domestic ticket, but I quickly learned that a ticket for foreign travel could not even be purchased until I had an official U.S. passport. I quickly completed my application and submitted it at the local post office. Thankfully, my application was quickly processed and I was able to provide a passport number for purchasing the ticket before it was too late. My destination was Thailand, but when I landed in China for my layover I realized that I was no longer dealing with the U.S. Transportation

Security Administration (TSA). Armed soldiers demanded to see my passport. They examined my picture and compared it to my face and asked me where I was headed. That passport served as my identification for the entire trip; I very carefully cared for it and was never out and about without it.

Purity can be likened to having a passport that displays godly wisdom. It identifies the heavenly nationality of the traveler and gives access to the modes of transportation that enable arrival at one's destination. The primary indicator of true wisdom—which has its source in God, is that of purity. When James identifies purity as the first attribute of wisdom he is connecting it to a holy life. The pursuit of wisdom is the pursuit of God's way of living which always falls within the parameters of purity. This demands a rejection of tainted worldly philosophies and sinful practices in favor of a biblical worldview and righteous living.

The journey to wisdom is not even a possibility until stopping at the Cross of Calvary. The depravity of Man's sins have caused him to veer so far off the path toward wisdom, that he has no bearings to correct his course. The wages of sin bring with it horrible consequences that rob, steal and destroy the purpose for which mankind was created. God's laws serve as a mirror for humanity, reflecting the consequences of sin. Man has repeatedly violated the laws of God. Justice demands that idolatrous, blasphemous, adulterous, lying, stealing, murderous, covetous sinners receive divine retribution for their despicable deeds. Man's sins demand hell as payment for his unrepentant rebellion.

> The journey to wisdom is not even a possibility until stopping at the Cross of Calvary.

God the Father in His boundless mercy recognized the desperate need for the redemption of His creation. He gave His only Son, Jesus Christ, as a ransom—in order to rescue mankind from the consequences of their sins. Christ did not deserve to die—for He had no sins of His own. He is divinely pure. Yet He voluntarily took on the sins of humanity when His blood was shed, serving as the atonement for sinful Man. This makes the gift of eternal life possible to all who will repent and believe in His forgiveness. The power of the Cross of Christ is so magnificent that those who believe can be made "the righteousness of God in Him" (2 Corinthians 5:21).

The only hope for sinful mankind to become pure is through salvation in Christ. This is why the journey to wisdom cannot even begin without a stop at the Cross. It is there that the fear of Lord begins, where heavenly citizenship is secured, and a repentant sinner is sealed with the Holy Spirit.

Repentance is a key element in understanding the purity of wisdom. Wisdom is not a self-help plan for a better life, but the only way to live the life which God intended. Unless the tainted humanism of the world is rejected it is impossible to be traveling in the right direction. Repentance corrects the course direction for the traveler giving him solid footing which makes the journey to wisdom possible.

A STARTLING CONTRAST

Throughout the entire book of Proverbs a contrast is made between the righteous and the wicked. The wicked are foolish and lean toward folly, but the righteous are wise and exhibit positive behavior. The morality of the individual is given as the key indicator of wisdom. While wisdom begins with the fear of the Lord, the foolish are in perpetual pursuit of mischief and wickedness (Proverbs 9:10; Psalm 111:10; Proverbs 10:23; Psalm 73:3).

Of particular emphasis in the book of Proverbs is the importance of marital faithfulness. It is very clear that the integrity of the marriage vow must be preserved both before and after the marriage takes place. Proverbs 5:15-23 describes marriage as the opportunity for fully enjoying a satisfying sexual relationship. With that description comes a rational argument against violating the sacredness of the marriage bed (Hebrews 13:4). God is aware and will hold the individual accountable for his or her actions. Sexual immorality is referred to as great folly (stupidity).

Immorality is a huge obstacle on the journey to wisdom. It is impossible to pursue both wisdom and immoral behavior. Proverbs chapter seven describes the intersection of an immoral woman with a man who falls into the simple category pursuing immorality. The simple one is referred to in Proverbs 7:7 as "void of understanding." He is certainly not thinking with his head and does not grasp the severity of what he is actively going after.

The immoral woman is lying in wait for easy prey and using clever language and seduction to convince the simple that integrity is not important. In the end, the simple one learns that "Her house is the way to hell, going down to the chambers of death"(Proverbs 7:27). The tragic consequences of surrendering to a wicked woman is illustrated in Proverbs 7:26, "For she hath cast down many wounded: yea, many strong men have been slain by her."

How Sex in the Culture Affects the Journey

A definite link exists between a commitment to sexual purity and wisdom. So many simple ones have detoured off the path toward wisdom because they became entrapped in immoral thoughts and behaviors. It is impossible to pursue both wisdom and immoral behavior. They stand in complete juxtaposition to one another. The highway to wisdom is littered with the scattered remains of those who surrendered to the seductions of immorality.

This is of particular concern in our current culture. Attitudes and practices toward sex across the spectrum of society are bleeding into the Church; the philosophies and practices of many believers are being affected. The National Campaign to Prevent Teen and Unplanned Pregnancy conducted an extensive nation-wide survey in 2009. The results revealed that 88 percent of unmarried adults between the ages 18-29 had engaged in sex. More disturbing, however, was the claim by this same survey that evangelicals in the same bracket were at 80 percent. If this statistic is accurate it shows that the believers are not much different than the non-believers in the area of sexual purity.

Grey Matter Research and Consulting in conjunction with the National Association of Evangelicals conducted a survey of around 1,007 evangelical young adults between the ages of 18 and 29 in 2012. Their results were not as severe and revealed that 44 percent of those surveyed had been sexually active. The disturbing revelation is that both of these surveys show a trend that even evangelical believers are not guarding their sexual purity as they should (when half or more of the young adults surveyed admit it).

Philosophies and not only behaviors are proving problematic in this area as well. Christian Mingle, an online Christian dating service, revealed in its 2014 State of Dating in America report that nearly two-thirds of Christians are willing to have casual sex before marriage. This prompted a Charisma News article titled "Sexual Atheism" in reference to so many Christians who are unwilling to acknowledge God's direction regarding sexual activity.

The trend in philosophy goes even deeper when it comes to the millennial generation. Nearly three out of four millennials think cohabitation is a good idea. And just over half of them think that consensual "safe" sex by teens is okay. The second half of Romans chapter one describes the evolution of a reprobate society. The phrase "reprobate mind" found in Romans 1:28 is clearly connected to the rejection of God's authority in favor of the false religion of humanism. Man became the final authority and God's ways were rejected.

The clearest evidence of a reprobate society is the embracing of homosexuality (vv. 26-27). The current society is not interested in only allowing homosexuality, but also promoting it. The modern-day progressives will only stop when it is not only accepted but also approved of legally. That goal was achieved in June of 2015 when the Supreme Court of the United States ruled that homosexual marriage was a constitutional right and the institution established by God on the sixth day of Creation was altered to fit the degenerate morality of the current culture.

The reprobate mind also leads to some very ludicrous decisions. Ever since the Supreme Court of the United States altered the definition of marriage, a transgender conflict has sprung up across the land on local, state and federal levels. With the redefinition of marriages comes a new progressive quest for fluidity in gender assignment and confusion as to who should use which bathrooms. The reprobate mind is truly depraved and leads society toward the implementation of policies that don't make a lot of sense.

It is evident that the trend in our culture is and has been for quite some time moving toward embracing sexual immorality. It also seems that within the ranks of believers there is a backlash against the purity movement of the 1990s and early 2000s. In some instances, well-meaning practices became hard-line legalism that left a bitter taste in the mouths of many Christians, causing them to throw the "baby out with the bathwater" in regard to the standards of purity.

I can testify personally to the impact of some of the great teachings that arose from that time period. They had a significant impact on my young life and helped strengthen my resolve toward guarding the sacredness of sex in marriage. The struggle in the lives of believers for sexual purity is real and very pertinent to the pursuit of wisdom.

DESIRE RIGHTEOUSNESS

If the journey to wisdom is to be made the traveler must pursue purity. Wisdom is breaking free from the foolishness of sinful practices and embracing God's precepts—which includes a lifestyle that is pure. Christ alone offers the starting point for purity. The contrast between wickedness and righteousness is potent and only the righteous can be wise.

The road to wisdom is first pure and must begin at the Cross. Progress on the journey demands the cultivation of a desire for righteousness. This must be actively pursued to combat against the lure of wickedness which brings the journey toward wisdom to a screeching halt.

POINTS TO PONDER

- Have you put your faith in Christ for salvation and the cleansing of sin? In order to achieve wisdom purity must come first—which is only possible through the cleansing power of Christ.

- Do you revere the sacredness of sex within marriage in both philosophy and actions?

- Everyone has desires. Do you have a desire for righteousness?

Chapter Fourteen

⚓

"Put a Knife to Thy Throat"

*When thou sittest to eat with a ruler, consider
diligently what is before thee: And put a knife to thy
throat, if thou be a man given to appetite.*
Proverbs 23:1-2

I LOVE FOOD. I don't know about you, but I like to eat. My son Josiah does too, and he is particularly fond of meat. He's an enthusiastic carnivore! When he was still a preschooler we had a plate of barbeque for dinner one night. We had an array of ribs, brisket and chicken wings. Josiah's mouth was drooling the second he sat down at the table. He was ready for some meat! As soon as we said "Amen" after thanking God for our bounty, he jumped up on his seat and reached over and started grabbing some food. He quickly picked up a chicken wing coated with Tabasco sauce—before we could stop him. At that age, he had the unique habit of licking his meat. As soon as he did that, his little tongue was on fire! He thought that sticking it out and blowing on it would help. Nevertheless, our meal was suddenly interrupted by my son yelling, "Hot!" followed by raspberry sounds as he tried to cool his tongue by blowing on it.

Josiah was seated next to me and I found this to be absolutely hilarious. My wife, however, wasn't as amused and told me to help him. So I did the first thing that came to mind; I gave him a cup of water. He immediately took the cup, stuck his tongue out, and dowsed his tongue with water. In the process, he also soaked himself and his area of the table. Now he had another problem and was yelling, "Hot!" followed by raspberry sounds as he tried to cool his tongue. Then followed by shouting, "Wet!" This pattern of yelling, "Hot!" and "Wet! continued until my wife was able to get me to stop rolling on the floor and laughing. We were then able to help our son drink more water (which seemed to do the trick).

I am not a food connoisseur who likes to eat fancy meals. Mainly, because my experience has been that you just get a little bit of food on your plate. That's supposed to be a delicacy? In my world, quantity trumps classy. Give me a buffet any day and I will be happy. I'll never forget when some of my college friends and I had the privilege of introducing a fellow classmate to Chinese food. We were in the middle of a tour around the country stopping at all kinds of restaurants. One day someone suggested we try a Chinese buffet. This classmate had never eaten Chinese food (American-style that is) and had convinced himself he wouldn't like it. It sounded like a bunch of rice to him and he didn't want to spend money on it. Finally, we persuaded him to join us. He reluctantly agreed. Because he had pre-paid for his meal, he filled up a plate.

As he began to eat you could see the transformation taking place on his face as he began to realize how good the food was. That night he downed seven heaping platefuls of Chinese buffet food. That was in Chicago. A few days later, that same student and I were rooming together in Seattle. While getting dressed for the day, I could hear the struggle he was having to get his pants buttoned. A few seconds later there was a "bing" sound as that button flew off and grazed my head in its flight path.

What do Tabasco chicken wings and a Chinese buffet have to do with wisdom? A powerful connection can be found between wisdom and our appetites. Not only appetites for food, but appetites for righteousness or wickedness. Appetite plays a significant role in determining the direction that a person will take. An appetite for righteousness will result in blessings (Matthew 5:6), while an appetite for wickedness will result in hardships (Proverbs 13:15).

AN APPETITE FOR RIGHTEOUSNESS

Biblical Daniel is an excellent example of someone who had an appetite for righteousness. In the book of Daniel chapter one, the four Hebrew children (Daniel, Shadrack, Meshack, and Abednego) find themselves in captivity to a wicked king, King Nebuchadnezzar in Babylon. Their captivity was not one of hardship as slaves working in a field, but as youth being trained as future counselors to the king. Due to their potential they were afforded access to food directly from the king's table. Yet Daniel purposed in his heart that he would not defile himself with the king's meat or drink (Daniel 1:8). As a result he, along with his three friends put in for a menu substitution. Instead of the fine delicacies from the king's table, they only wanted to eat vegetables, porridge and drink only water.

Why would these young men refuse to eat the king's food and drink? As Jews, there were certainly dietary restrictions that they followed—but surely there were at least some kosher meats that they could have eaten without violating the Mosaic Law. As a pagan society, it is also very likely that much of the food from the king's table had been first offered as a sacrifice to a false god. If that is true, then Daniel and his friends would not have wanted to defile themselves. While the Scriptures are not definitive for the reasons they rejected the king's rich delicacies, the entire scenario is beautifully illustrated in Proverbs 23:1-8:

> "When thou sittest to eat with a ruler, consider diligently what is before thee: And put a knife to thy throat, if thou be a man given to appetite. Be not desirous of his dainties: for they are deceitful meat. Labour not to be rich: cease from thine own wisdom. Wilt thou set thine eyes upon that which is not? for riches certainly make themselves wings; they fly away as an eagle toward heaven. Eat thou not the bread of him that hath an evil eye, neither desire thou his dainty meats: For as he thinketh in his heart, so is he: Eat and drink, saith he to thee; but his heart is not with thee. The morsel which thou hast eaten shalt thou vomit up, and lose thy sweet words."

Daniel was so purposed in his heart that he would not allow any influence in his life that would defile him. He wasn't about to start eating from the table of the king and put himself in a position where he might be willing to compromise himself. Daniel chapter ten vividly describes a twenty-one day fast that Daniel completed. That particular fast is often called The Daniel Fast.

> "In those days I Daniel was mourning three full weeks. I ate no pleasant bread, neither came flesh nor wine in my mouth, neither did I anoint myself at all, till three whole weeks were fulfilled" (Daniel 10:3).

The passage above makes it clear that Daniel did begin to eat other things and did not remain a vegetarian. The Daniel Fast, has become very popular and is emulated by many believers. Daniel's fast included staying away from meat, sweets, and wine—the very foods which he refused to partake of in chapter one. It seems that Daniel found that in his youthful stage of life that an appetite for righteousness demanded he go without certain things. The pursuit of wisdom passes through spiritual boot camp; the flesh is denied and the spiritual life is strengthened.

AN APPETITE FOR WICKEDNESS
Another biblical character stands in stark contrast to Daniel in regard to appetite—Samson, the strongest man to have ever lived. Judges chapter fourteen relates an incident in Samson's life that illustrates his appetite. Samson was interested in marrying a Philistine woman and on his way to visit her, he was attacked by a lion. The Spirit of the Lord came upon him and he was able to easily kill the lion with his bare hands.

Samson told no one about the incident. After some time he returned to see the carcass of the dead lion. To his delight he found that some bees had made a hive inside the carcass of the dead animal and it was now teeming with honey. He gladly ate some of the honey and shared it with his parents (leaving out the particular details about where he found it). He even used the entire lion incident as a riddle that became a wager against the Philistines at his wedding.

Before Samson's mother was born, an angel told her that she would bear a son. She was also informed that he would be a Nazarite from his birth to his death (Judges 13:7). Numbers 6:1-21 give clear instructions for the Nazarite to follow and expressly forbids three things. First, the Nazarite was not to consume any form of wine or alcohol. And to prevent any chance of intoxication they were not allowed to eat anything whatsoever off of the vine.

Second, the Nazarite was not to cut his hair but was to allow it to grow all the days of his consecration to the Lord. Samson is particularly famous for his long hair and the connection that it had to the source of his strength.

The final element of the Nazarite vow was not to come into contact with any dead body whatsoever and this is where the story of Samson and the lion becomes somewhat telling. Samson saw the honey inside the carcass of the dead lion and reached into it, took it out, ate some of it and shared it with his parents (without letting them know the source, of course).

It's not as if Samson was famished and needed the energy to continue his journey. No, he just wanted a snack. Samson's appetite was out of control and he violated his vow to God for a snack! The honey was okay, but where he got it from was wrong. He would have done well to remember Proverbs 25:16, "Hast thou found honey? Eat so much as is sufficient for thee, lest thou be filled therewith, and vomit it."

> In the pursuit of wisdom an appetite for righteousness must be cultivated.

Samson's physical appetite was symbolic of his persistent appetite for wickedness, particularly in regard to sexual immorality. Samson went after pagan ladies, sought prostitutes and fell into the seductions of Delilah—which ultimately led to his blindness and bondage. He was strong physically, but weak in spirit because he had an appetite for wickedness.

In the pursuit of wisdom an appetite for righteousness must be cultivated. No one is perfect and the battle of the fleshly sin nature is ongoing until the day we die. But it *is* possible to master the appetite through the power of the Holy Spirit and for an appetite for righteousness to prevail. The results for individuals who become mighty in spirit—like the prophet Daniel, will be to have the ability to endure any challenges or detours they may face on their journey to wisdom.

THE LURE OF WICKEDNESS

A lure of wickedness is prevalent in many places. Just like Lady Folly in chapter seven of Proverbs, it decks itself out with ornaments and makes itself appealing. Attractive images flash across screens or pop up in ads used as tantalizing bait—preying upon fleshly appetites, seeking to hook passersby.

I am familiar with a legend about how the Inuit Indians of the upper reaches of North America set a trap for wolves. Legend has it that they would sharpen a knife blade to a razor point and then cover the knife blade in the blood of an animal and freeze it. Multiple layers would be added to the blade creating a sort of blood popsicle.

The hunter would then find a location where the wolf would pass by and bury the handle of the knife in the snow with the blade exposed. When the wolf passed by and took the bait it would begin to lick the blood ice and continue to do so until the ice was gone and it was now feasting upon its own blood as the blade cut its mouth until the animal would bleed out and die.

Wickedness has the same lure. It calls to the simple attempting to lure them. Too often the simple follow after the wicked "as an ox goeth to the slaughter." Surrendering to carnal appetites will always bring pain and destruction—the tragic reward of fools.

Coke and Pepsi have been rivals in the soft drink industry for decades. That rivalry peaked in the late 1970s and early 1980s when Pepsi's market share began to gain on Coke's. Up to that point, Coke had dominated the soft drink industry. Part of the reason for Pepsi's market share increase was due to the success of a blind taste test marketing campaign.

Pepsi conducted blind taste tests all around the country and promoted the results that were found. The television commercials would, of course, always show that the tasters preferred the sweet, smooth taste of Pepsi over the harsher Coke. (In reality, it was true that people did prefer Pepsi in the taste tests.)

This soft-drink upheaval began to cause panic within the upper echelons of the Coca-Cola Company. If people's tastes were changing then perhaps it was time to make some changes to the secret soda formula (that had remained unchanged for decades).

Scientists at the company began to tinker with the formula until they produced a concoction that was sweeter and smoother. They conducted their own taste tests and manipulated the new formula until they had something that would beat Pepsi in extensive taste tests around the world.

When the Coca-Cola Company was confident they had what it would take to outmatch Pepsi, they released it under a name, "New Coke." It was an utter failure! People revolted against the new flavor and demanded that the old one be returned. Eventually, the company conceded and returned the old flavor under the name, "Coca-Cola Classic." The experience was so terrible that they kept the word "Classic" in the name for *two decades* to ensure consumer trust.

The reason for this revolt goes back to Coca Cola's flawed taste tests. The majority of people do not drink soft drinks one sip at a time. The small amount of the new Coke that the taste tests offered did not match the practices of the average person. Many people like to drink soda in 12 or 20-ounce cans and bottles or in a giant gulp size from a convenience store. The sweeter taste of Pepsi won in a taste test, but it was too sweet in large quantities, and many consumers preferred the taste of the classic formula of Coke. Not as sweet in a taste test, but better by the glass.

Wickedness will often win in a taste test (Hebrews 11:25). But a belly full of it will turn the stomach. A life of wickedness will reap the results of folly and only bring pain and destruction. It is the bread of deceit that tastes sweet, but after the initial taste, it turns to gravel in the mouth (Proverbs 20:17).

Lady Folly promises that her stolen waters of immorality are sweet and that the secret deeds of sexual sin are pleasant. When tasting a small amount that may be true, but after a full glass is consumed it will leave bitter gall in the belly. This is the inevitable result of surrendering to carnal appetites; it prevents a life of wisdom.

> "Stolen water is sweet, and bread *eaten* in secret is pleasant. But he does not know that the dead *are* there, *That* her guests *are* in the depths of hell" (Proverbs 9:17-18).

A Passion for Righteousness

Standing in stark contrast to wickedness is the cry of wisdom as she calls and says, "Come eat of my bread and drink of the wine which I have mingled. Forsake the foolish and live and go in the way everlasting" (Proverbs 9:6). Because wisdom is based in the fear of the Lord its pursuit demands a passion for righteousness.

There is an adorable little weasel-like creature known as the stoat or ermine. This little creature has a chestnut coat of fur in the summer, but when the winter rolls around his coat turns a brilliant white and when that happens it is referred to as the ermine. This little creature is very concerned with the cleanliness of his coat and as a result, it has been a very prized fur throughout the history of Northern Europe. The white fur of the ermine became associated with royalty and during the time of Edward III could only be worn by royalty.

Tales of how hunters of old captured the ermine for its valuable pelt, illustrates the determination to maintain the purity of its coat. The hunter would first discover the den of the ermine and wait for it to go out on a hunt. Then the hunter would scatter grime and debris all around the entrance of the den. Upon doing so the hounds would be released and the instinct of the ermine was to return to the safety of the den. Upon arriving and discovering that he could not enter the den without soiling his precious white coat, the ermine would refuse the safety of the den and would instead turn and face the dogs, willing to fight to the death if necessary to protect the purity of his coat.

That scenario depicts a passion for maintaining purity—which is exactly the appetite needed for righteousness. Those in the pursuit of wisdom must exhibit such dedication. Wisdom demands a passionate pursuit of purity. So if you're a person given to appetite, "Put a knife to thy throat." Or as Jesus so brazenly stated to make his point, "And if thy right eye offend thee, pluck it out, and cast *it* from thee: for it is profitable for thee that one of thy members should perish, and not *that* thy whole body should be cast into hell." In other words, do whatever is necessary to escape the lure of wickedness and pursue righteousness instead.

Dedication and passion fuel the desire for wisdom. When anyone—particularly youth, develop an appetite for godly righteousness, goading will not be needed on the journey to wisdom. The destination will be actively pursued because a passion for the things of God go hand in hand with a desire to obtain wisdom.

Points to Ponder

- Do you understand that an appetite for wickedness leads to destruction?

- Are you cultivating an appetite for righteousness? What things can you do to starve the flesh and feed the spirit?

- Can you honestly say that you have a passion for righteousness?

Chapter Fifteen

⚓

Character Counts

"THIS COULD BE the one!" My mind was racing as my dad told me that a friend of his was selling a car. It was the summer before my final year at Bible college and I had been praying for a car. I hadn't needed one throughout the previous years, but as ministry opportunities were increasing I felt as though the Lord wanted me to have one.

My home is in Massachusetts, but I was enrolled in a college in Texas. I knew that the car needed to get me from point A to point B in one piece. I had only two requests for the Lord as I prayed: A working air conditioner and a working cassette player. (That last part of the prayer really dates me.) I was so confident in the provision of the Lord that I didn't buy airplane tickets for the trip back to college. I persuaded my sister and another young man at my home church who were attending the same college that I would have a car and they could drive back with me; so they didn't buy tickets either.

I was convinced that I should not go into debt for any car that I might purchase. I had saved around two thousand dollars and was trusting that the Lord would help me find something. That July, my father told me about a car that a friend of his from work was selling. This friend seemed to think that it would be a good fit for me. I was ecstatic when my father told me the make and model of the car. It was a Ford Mustang! Immediately vanity began to take over as I contemplated having the coolest car on campus. Having a Mustang would definitely make an impression. My father asked me if I wanted him to bring it home from work so I could look it over. "Yeah, of course," was my immediate response.

It's funny how your mind can create all kinds of visions of grandeur. I was completely convinced that this was going to be *the* provision of the Lord. The price was less than my budget. I had plenty of time to get things ready for my trip back to school. This must be it. Then I watched as my father drove the car up our driveway when returning home from work the next night. All my hopes seemed to evaporate into oblivion with one look. What was once probably a great sports car now looked like a dilapidated hunk of junk. The paint was peeling, there was duct tape covering holes in the body that had rotted out and one of the windows didn't work. But it was still a Mustang! I thought that perhaps upon closer examination there was still hope that it might work out. (Of course there wasn't.) It was a two-door car with a smaller than average trunk which would never work for three college kids and their luggage.

The problem was that not only were my options limited because of my budget and my conviction that I should not borrow any money, but time was running out. We all needed to be at school by the middle of August. I debated as to whether I should take my chances and just take the car as it was. My father's counsel was that I should remember that "Every good and perfect gift comes from above" and that I would know when it was from the Lord by using that criteria.

I received his counsel and turned down the Mustang, but my anxiety began to grow. I still trusted that God would provide, but it sure seemed He was taking his sweet time about it as the calendar had now changed to August. I would need to report to school in just two weeks. The first day of August that year was a Sunday. I went to church as usual. I don't remember the message from that day, but I do remember what happened to me after the pastor closed in prayer and said, "Amen!" I was seated behind a gentleman who was relatively new to our church. He also attended prayer meetings and he knew that I was praying that the Lord would provide me with a car. He turned around right after the closing prayer and asked, "Hey, have you got a car yet?"

I sheepishly replied, "No, not yet" as I stood to leave the meeting.

His next words, literally, almost knocked me off my feet as he quickly replied, "The Lord wants me to give you my car."

I wasn't sure how to respond, but I think I might have gone a little pale as I said, "Are you sure?"

He said, "Yes, we'll talk about it soon" and with that he left.

I was in a state of amazement and overwhelmed. I remember my grand-mother, who had heard the conversation, looked over at me and asked if I was all right. I sat back down and for several minutes. I was in complete awe of what the Lord had done for me. I knew exactly what car he was talking about. He had a beautiful red Toyota 4Runner with only 28,000 miles on it. There was more than enough luggage space and it was loaded with extras like a moonroof and four-wheel drive. The AC worked fantastically and there was an audio system with a cassette player and surround sound. The best part was that "free" fit perfectly into my budget!

I drove to Texas in style that year. The Lord had sent a "good and perfect gift" and increased my faith in Him as my Provider. My first day back at the dorm one of my friends commented that I definitely had "the hottest car at school." It was a reliable car that served me well for ten years. On the journey to wisdom, it is important to have reliable transportation. It is likely that the old Mustang would have broken down on the road somewhere between Connecticut and Texas, but the 4Runner was reliable. On the journey to wisdom, character will serve as the mode of transportation and will reliably carry the driver to his or her destination.

CHARACTER'S ROLE

The book of Proverbs emphasizes the importance of excellent character. Martin Luther King Jr. famously dreamed of a day when his children would "…not be judged by the color of their skin but by the content of their character." The book of Proverbs is the expression of that sentiment. It completely defines people by their behavior.

The development of character in a person's life (in particular—youth), is the greatest catalyst on the journey to wisdom. It is like rocket fuel. A character deficiency is like adding water to a gas tank. It will bring the journey to a quick halt and require the fuel lines in the tank to be cleaned. When character is developed and refined in a godly manner, the strength of that character will provide endurance to reach the desired destination of God-given wisdom.

Character is not determined at birth, it is developed. All of humanity has an innate ability to develop godly character. After all, mankind was created "in the image and likeness of God" (Genesis 1:26-27). This is an inherent hard-wired trait with the capacity to cultivate and express godly attributes. But sin has corrupted God's creation placing roadblocks on the road to wisdom.

These roadblocks cannot be removed without the activation of God's grace through saving faith.

Individuals with virtuous character have the endurance necessary to successfully navigate the journey to attain wisdom. The messages in the book of Proverbs continuously contrast a strong character with that of a weak character. Of course, godly character is emphasized. It provides a person with a reliable means of transportation needed when traveling. The godly and righteous are diligent and disciplined. They consistently exhibit self-control and can delay gratification. Their attributes can be likened to the high-performance qualities of my loaded 4Runner. But the ungodly lack those positive traits and are more like a sad heap of rubble, comparable to the duct-taped Ford Mustang my father's friend was trying to sell.

THE CASE FOR CHARACTER

The high value of character from a biblical viewpoint is not isolated to the book of Proverbs. It can be found throughout the entire Bible. One of the most powerful passages emphasizing strong character is found in 2 Peter chapter one. Verse ten gives the challenge to "…give diligence to make your calling and election sure: for if ye do these things, ye shall never fall." That is, Peter is writing to believers telling them that if they will do certain things it will build their lives in ways that will prevent a fall (or failure) along life's journey.

Peter presents eight things in specific order which believers can diligently add to their lives to build themselves up. The passage starts by describing the results of saving faith. Salvation enables us to partake in God's divine nature. It gives us an enhanced ability to build godly character.

> "According as his divine power hath given unto us all things that pertain unto life and godliness, through the knowledge of him that hath called us to glory and virtue: Whereby are given unto us exceeding great and precious promises: that by these ye might be partakers of the divine nature, having escaped the corruption that is in the world through lust.
>
> And beside this, giving all diligence, add to your faith virtue; and to virtue knowledge; and to knowledge temperance; and to temperance patience; and to patience godliness; And to godliness brotherly kindness; and to brotherly kindness charity. For if these things be in you, and abound, they

make you that ye shall neither be barren nor unfruitful in the knowledge of our Lord Jesus Christ" (2 Peter 1:3-8).

A Christian's walk of reliability takes place when faith grows into what the King James Version of the Bible translates as "virtue." The word virtue can be literally translated as "manliness (valor)" or "excellence." The use of the term "virtue" most often refers to moral purity and an excellent character. Christ our Lord was full of virtue. It emanated from Him. When the woman with the issue of blood touched the hem of His garment, Jesus knew that "virtue had gone out from Him" to heal her (Mark 5:30).

Perhaps virtue can best be understood as the energy, influence and power sourced from God transferred into the lives of believers—which enables them to live the right way evidenced by having godly character. This takes character from a simplistic understanding of the development of certain habits in life into something more lasting and more powerful. Righteous character is a supernatural relationship with Almighty God in which His virtue is imparted into the believer.

> The believer's destiny is to reflect the character of Jesus Christ.

Godly character can be imitated but in its most genuine state it is an expression of the work of the Holy Spirit in the life of a believer. I will never forget one young man I met at Bible college. He exemplified this principal so well. He was saved early in the summer and had already enrolled in Bible college by August. His knowledge of the Scriptures was akin to being illiterate. He had not grown up in church. He had never studied the Scriptures (as many at our school had).

Nevertheless, I found myself having conversations with him in which he would speak about various topics. I would point out or quote a Scripture passage to show him that what he was saying was biblically sound. He would often say something like, "Really, I didn't know the Bible said that." It always fascinated me that he knew nothing of the Scriptures and yet was somehow able to comprehend and assimilate its truths and principles. Others at the school also found he had an extraordinary understanding of things related to Scripture. He exemplified virtue! He was so close to the Lord, even with his infant faith—that he could express virtuous character.

The remaining traits addressed in 2 Peter chapter one are temperance, patience, godliness, brotherly kindness and charity. We often associate those traits with good character. Indeed, they are part of genuine character that flows from the influence of God. Does character count? Absolutely. It builds reliability into the believer's journey. James 4:17 makes it clear that knowledge without appropriate action is sin: "Therefore, to him who knows to do good and does not do it, to him it is sin." Virtue, or character, produces that right action in a person's life.

It Is Your Destiny!

The *Star Wars* saga made the term "destiny" very popular. It has had a ripple effect on our culture. This very trendy buzzword has also been picked up by many churches and preachers. Preachers often throw the word "destiny" into their sermons. It is most commonly used to imply that God has some special and amazing plans for an individual's life.

That principle is fine. But sadly it is often misconstrued to mean that a person can somehow fulfill that destiny by being in a worship service with just the right atmosphere. It seems that some preachers are implying that by being in the right service with an uplifting song being played—a congregant can achieve a single "moment" in which he or she can fulfill that "destiny" and "change the world."

A true biblical understanding of destiny does not reduce the word to a mystical term that must be discovered by undertaking a personal quest. God has a plan for every believer's life and that plan is as unique as the individual—a predetermined destiny for every believer (which is often ignored). The apostle Paul clearly cited in Romans 8:29, that the foreknowledge of God predestines the believer to be conformed to the "image of his Son."

The believer's destiny *is* to reflect the character of Jesus Christ. As the character of Christ is developed a person's capacity to fulfill his or her unique plan ("destiny") is enhanced. Destiny preaching is only good if it goes on to tell believers how to truly attain that destiny. It is achieved when godly character is built into a believer's life. Not only is character necessary, "It is your destiny!"

Building Character

While godly character stems from a relationship with Christ it is important to add, or build it into a believer's life. The book of Proverbs gives significant focus to character in general. There are three areas of character emphasized in Proverbs that can be developed, even from an early age: Diligence, discipline and delayed gratification. These areas can have a significant impact on character for better or for worse.

DILIGENCE

The way a person approaches work reveals much about his or her character. There are two types of workers in continual contrast within Proverbs—the diligent and the lazy. Each has distinguishing characteristics and predictable outcomes. The diligent worker is praised continually and is given the expectation of positive outcomes for hard work. The lazy person is admonished to change his ways or suffer the consequences.

Diligent workers are illustrated in Proverbs by using an insect—the ant. Proverbs 6:6-8 serves as a rebuke to the lazy and describes some of the diligent characteristics of the little ant. "Go to the ant, thou sluggard; consider her ways, and be wise: Which having no guide, overseer, or ruler, provideth her meat in the summer, and gathereth her food in the harvest."

The ant is a responsible self-motivated worker and does not require supervision to undertake and complete tasks. (A diligent person sees what needs doing and does it.)

Diligence is also thorough in its way of working and living. Diligent people think through the work at hand and ensure that it is done properly to reap a positive result; they are thoughtful. "The thoughts of the diligent tend only to plenteousness; but of every one that is hasty only to want" (Proverbs 21:5).

God demonstrated this thoroughness in creation. Before finishing up on day six He examined all of His creation and it was all good except for one thing: It wasn't good for man to be alone so he created woman. Then everything was VERY GOOD! God demonstrated thoughtfulness and thoroughness even in His creation.

Diligent workers are resourceful and ensure quality on the job. The slothful waste what they have, "but the substance of a diligent man is precious" (Proverbs 12:27). While the lazy man is wasting, the diligent man is utilizing every resource at his disposal to efficiently accomplish tasks.

Diligence is starkly contrasted by the lazy man, which is a trait of a scorner. Remember, in Proverbs there are two types of lazy people. The first type is the one who works, but does a sloppy job with an attitude of indifference. The work he does often needs to be redone and requires close supervision. This is why the diligent most often need to supervise lazy people. "The hand of the diligent shall bear rule: but the slothful shall be under tribute" (Proverbs 12:24).

The second kind of lazy person described in Proverbs is the one who simply does not work. He always has an excuse for not working, sleeps a lot and is so indolent that he won't even take his hand out of his pocket to feed himself (Proverbs 26:13-15).

A diligent character needs to be cultivated and the habit of laziness must be resisted. The best method for fostering and encouraging diligence is by having a reward system. While the reward should not be the ultimate motivation for putting forth a best effort, it is certainly a viable incentive to help encourage diligence and discourage laziness. The diligent man is assured that his diligence will promote him to a point of standing before kings and not just common folk (Proverbs 22:29).

The diligent reap the rewards of their efforts, but the lazy miss out. Why would someone exhibit diligence without the promise or expectation of a reward? If the lazy reap the same benefits as the diligent why bother trying? There is indeed a reward for diligence, but poverty is the end result of laziness (Proverbs 20:13 ; Proverbs 14:23).

Almighty God rewards diligence. He promises to be the "rewarder of those who diligently seek Him" (Hebrews 11:6). The Lord Jesus Himself declared in Revelation 22:12 that He was coming quickly and would "reward every one according to his work."

SELF-DISCIPLINE

A second very important area for character development is self-discipline. The ability to discipline oneself and demonstrate self-control is lauded in the book of Proverbs. The individual who can control his emotions and temper is praised as being even better than a mighty warrior who can take the city. "He that is slow to anger is better than the mighty; and he that ruleth his spirit than he that taketh a city" (Proverbs 16:32).

In contrast, the person who lacks discipline and self-control is like an unfortified city susceptible to attacks by the enemy (Proverbs 25:28).

The current culture in general reflects more of an unfortified city than that of a mighty warrior. Teachers are facing a significant rise in behavioral issues in the classroom from elementary through high school levels by up to 68 percent according to recent studies. This rise in behavioral difficulties has led to a decrease in academic instruction and an increase in time spent on discipline. The socio-economic status of the students didn't alter the results of the studies. Those from poor neighborhoods were just as undisciplined as those from rich neighborhoods.

A lack of self-discipline will always create problems. When a person's temper is not controlled and anger is allowed to burst out it can create significant health problems and relationship problems. Consider the problem of road rage which was responsible for 218 murders and 12,610 injuries over a seven year period. AAA released a study in 2016 revealing that nearly 80 percent of all drivers express anger, aggression or rage. Why do so many people lose it when someone cuts them off on the road? They lack discipline and the ability to control themselves.

Then there's the rise of "sports rage." This is the phenomenon in which parents, in particular, lose their temper at youth games and commit acts of violence against other parents, coaches, players or sports officials. Some become so enraged over a "game" that they murder! There is a reason that Proverbs 22:24 advises, "Make no friendship with an angry man; and with a furious man thou shalt not go." Anger is excess baggage that will hinder the journey to wisdom. Lighten the load with self-discipline.

Humans were created as emotional beings distinguishing mankind from the rest of creation which also serves as a powerful link to the Creator (who also expresses emotion). Man's will is strong and does not have to be controlled by emotions. Self-control is one of the fruits of the spirit bringing with it the strength to temper the emotions.

My wife and I are purposeful in the way we instruct our children in this area, particularly our boys. Children must learn how to properly express their emotions. Our constant goal is to teach them to control those emotions. They understand that when we say, "Self-control!" It is a cue for them to pause and allow their will to overcome their emotions. It's not always easy but they can do it. They are young boys now but soon they will be young men and we want them to be mighty in spirit which demands self-control.

Perhaps no other area in life demands discipline more than when using the tongue. The apostle James spoke of the dangers that the tongue can cause when it is allowed to run wild. Truly the tongue left to itself, will be ablaze with hellfire. "Death and life are in the power of the tongue: and they that love it shall eat the fruit thereof" (Proverbs 18:21).

The power of words must be wielded responsibly and deliberately. Loose lips are an indication of foolishness. It is only the fool that utters every word that comes into his head. The wise man keeps his thoughts to himself until after he has thought them through; very often he leaves his thoughts unsaid (Proverbs 29:11). "Even a fool, when he holdeth his peace, is counted wise: and he that shutteth his lips is esteemed a man of understanding" (Proverbs 17:28).

While it seems that some individuals have foot-shaped-mouths, no one is condemned to a life of endless chatter. Self-control in the words that are spoken can be achieved. The brain can be engaged before the mouth begins to speak. It is no coincidence that the first evidence of the Holy Spirit baptism in the book of Acts was His control of the believer's tongue.

James chapter 3 is very clear that if you can master the tongue you can in turn, master the entire body. The power of God's Spirit is indeed present to give self-control in the spoken word to those who are willing to surrender to His discipline. Truly, "In the multitude of words there wanteth not sin: but he that refraineth his lips is wise" (Proverbs 10:19). Disciplining the tongue is an important element of success in journeying to wisdom.

Proverbs gives two separate warnings about a pothole in the road that can negatively affect discipline in the life of the traveler in regard to alcohol. In Proverbs 20:1 wine and strong drink are referenced as raging and a deceptive mocker. Chapter 23 verses 29-35 describe the drunkard and the trouble that he brings upon himself. Alcohol is a drug that has caused more death, chaos and destruction than any other substance known to mankind. Most recently, the Center for Disease Control released a study revealing that 1 in 10 deaths in the United States are related to alcohol somehow. Nothing good ever comes out of consuming alcohol.

Nearly all Christians would agree that drunkenness is a sin. However, many feel that it is acceptable to drink socially or in moderation. It is true that Jesus turned the water into wine and Paul told Timothy to "Use a little wine for thy stomach's sake" (1 Timothy 5:23). Just about every other biblical reference to alcohol is connected to drunkenness and a loss of self-control that leads to unwise choices. Noah became drunk after the flood and the end result was a curse on his family. Lot became a drunk and was guilty of incest with his daughters during his stupor, and the list goes on.

Those who would drink are admonished to be careful and curses are pronounced upon those who serve liquor to their neighbor. Those who refrained completely, like the Rechabites in Jeremiah 35, were blessed. The Nazarite distinguished himself as separated unto God not only by his long hair but also by his abstinence from alcohol.

One of the many problems with alcohol consumption is that it negatively affects discipline. Because of its ability to remove inhibitions, it has a tremendous potential to lead to a loss of self-control and rash decisions. That is one reason why strong warnings are given from wise leaders in order to avoid hazardous detours that can arise on the road to wisdom—detours that can cause total derailment or lengthy delays. Self-discipline and self-control are of utmost importance for a successful journey to wisdom and there's no room for taking risks or falling into potholes.

DELAYED GRATIFICATION

One final area of consideration for character development is the ability to delay gratification. Several attributes of wisdom are reflective of the principle of waiting for the best, instead of settling for the immediate. In 1965, Walter Mischel, a professor of psychology at Stanford University began a massive study that would come to be known as the Marshmallow Test. The study centered around analyzing the ability of preschoolers to delay gratification and then tracking them for the next several decades to see if it made a difference. The subjects of the study were offered a special treat, like a marshmallow, that they could eat right away if they wanted to, but with the caveat that if they waited until the instructor returned they would be given a second marshmallow to enjoy.

The marshmallow was placed on the table directly in front of the child and then the instructor left the room. The children were clearly informed that at any point they could stop the test by ringing a bell on the table at the sound of which the instructor would return and they could eat the marshmallow right away, but they would not get a second. The child would then be left alone with the tasty temptation for fifteen minutes—an eternity for preschoolers. For some, the temptation of the fluffy white treat in front of them was too much to resist and they rang the bell and ate the treat before the time was up. Others, however, were able to resist the urge to immediately consume the treat and lasted the entire timeframe and were rewarded with a second marshmallow.

The results of the initial study of the preschoolers are fascinating, in particular in regard to the creative techniques used by the children to help resist immediate temptation. Some would push the marshmallow close to the edge of the table as far away as possible—as if pushing the temptation away. Some would sing or play games with their hands or fingers to distract themselves and keep from thinking about the treat in front of them. However, the real power of the study was not in the immediate observations, but in the observations that came decades later.

Over the course of the fifty years since the study began it was discovered that the preschoolers who were able to delay gratification for the marshmallow had lower BMI, lower rates of addiction, lower rates of divorce and higher SAT scores. The study was conducted worldwide and the results were universal. The ability to delay gratification and wait for something more or better does factor into a more "successful" life. In fact, the study was able to predict with reasonable accuracy the likelihood of adult successes based on a preschooler's ability to delay gratification.

Proverbs paints a picture of the wise that reflects an ability to delay gratification. The wise will choose what is best not only for the present but also for the future and eternity. This sometimes requires the sacrifice of the temporal on the altar of the eternal which is the ultimate expression of delayed gratification. The journey to wisdom requires the ability to delay gratification.

The book of Proverbs addresses some significant areas of wisdom that require this ability to delay gratification. The area of debt and lifestyle fall into this category. Debt has become a vicious taskmaster in the modern economy, yet the Proverbs have some very strong warnings against it. We are told that "the borrower is servant to the lender" (Proverbs 22:7) and that getting into debt is an act "void of understanding" (Proverbs 17:18). How fascinating that a May 22, 2017 article on Nasdaq.com is titled, "Household Debt is Enslaving Americans."

The statistics on debt for everything from credit cards, cars, student loans, etc. are overwhelming. A significant driver of much of this debt is a lack of ability to delay gratification. Rather than work and save for items it is too easy to "buy now and pay later." The standard of living that many Americans support is filled with non-essentials that are considered to be necessities and they will accrue debt to maintain that standard.

The gospels relate an incident in which a rich young man came to Jesus desiring to be His disciple. He asked, "Good Master, what shall I do that I may inherit eternal life?" After a brief conversation the Lord saw his sincerity and loved him. He gave the young man this instruction, "One thing thou lackest: go thy way, sell whatsoever thou hast, and give to the poor, and thou shalt have treasure in heaven: and come, take up the cross, and follow me."

This statement was too much for the young man to handle. Because he had so many great possessions he left sad, unwilling to part with them (Mark 10:17-22). The rich young ruler didn't have any trouble doing what God wanted him to do. He had confessed to doing the right things his whole life. His problem was that he didn't want to lower his standard of living. This was his hindrance to following after Christ. He came looking for eternal life but missed it because he was unable to delay gratification of the flesh in the temporal to gain the eternal.

Too many people in this generation are neglecting the call of the Lord—to follow Him into ministry work or the mission field. Economics rule their decisions instead of a devotion to God's calling. The pay scale is often not enough in ministry work to support their desired standard of living; or they are so burdened with debt that they are slaves to their jobs in order to make the required payments. The journey to wisdom is a full-throttle pursuit of Christ, and the entanglement of the things of this world can cause stalling in the breakdown lane on the road to wisdom. Delay the gratification of the flesh in favor of eternal blessings.

Sexual purity has already been discussed in this book, but delayed gratification is a necessity in this area. I woke up on the morning of my wedding day a twenty-seven-year-old virgin. By the grace of God, my sexual purity was intact and presented as a honeymoon gift to my wife. This was not because I never faced temptation. Far from it! It was a result of delayed gratification. Far too many are eating their frosting before their cake instead of with it.

Popular honeymoon destinations are adding all kinds of attractions for bored couples to keep occupied. My wife and I went to Niagara Falls, but our destination was not at all our main interest. I think we saw the water falls once during our entire time there. We were far more interested in each other because we had waited for each other.

The Marshmallow Test also presented suggestions and techniques for increasing one's ability to delay gratification. One important technique is to develop the ability to envision your future self. This involves seeing what you would like to become or do and creating that picture in your mind as a stimulus to reach for and achieve that goal. I can see where this would apply to wisdom as well. Far too often we keep our eyes on the here and now and forget about "The Sweet By-and-By" as related in the popular classic Christian hymn. Delayed gratification demands vision, and without it the people perish (Proverbs 29:18).

MOLDED THROUGH MODELING

Character is something that is most often molded into a life. It is caught more than it is taught. That is why it is important to have positive role models who demonstrate godly character. One of the elements of character (virtue) is that it is transferable. That transference works both ways; the advice of the Psalmist in chapter 1 should be followed—completely avoid the wicked. Also, the apostle Paul warned in 1 Corinthians 15:33 that evil companions have a corrupting influence on character.

Remember, the journey to wisdom requires not only desire but strong leadership. Perhaps the most powerful form of leadership in this area is the modeling of godly character. Character will be taught through knowledge of right and wrong, but it will be shaped by actions.

> When godly character is displayed by those in a position of influence—it can be emulated by others. Teaching and modeling go hand-in-hand with developing character. Jesus called those who do and teach the commandments the greatest in the kingdom of heaven (Matthew 5:19).

Godly character equips an individual to pursue the journey to wisdom. It functions like a mode of transportation that can accelerate progress and provide reliability on the journey. The only question that remains is whether the person seeking wisdom is a driving a duct-taped Ford Mustang or a loaded 4Runner.

IN CONCLUSION

It is evident from what has been discussed that the path to wisdom is a lifetime journey. It has been said that the journey of a thousand miles begins with the first step. The journey to wisdom can begin right now with a first step. The journey must begin with the fear of the Lord and the understanding that wisdom is sourced from God and God alone.

Wisdom is available to all who will hear her call and respond appropriately—no matter where a person is positioned on the roadmap of life. It is a long, sometimes arduous journey that requires reliable transportation—strong character shaped by God's Word.

Delaying action is often the greatest hindrance on the journey toward wisdom. Lady Wisdom is calling and promises "...those who seek me early shall find me" (Proverbs 8:17). She desires that the simple would avoid all the potholes on the road to folly, and to get and stay on the road to wisdom (beginning in the early years of life).

It is never too early to hear the cry of wisdom. The promise to those who seek wisdom early in life is contrasted with those who delay and wait purposely—pursuing the way of fools. Throughout the book of Proverbs a dire warning is given to those who procrastinate and wait. Those who delayed starting the journey to wisdom lost their opportunity and it was too late; wisdom could not be found.

> "Then shall they call upon me, but I will not answer; they shall seek me early, but they shall not find me: For that they hated knowledge, and did not choose the fear of the LORD: They would none of my counsel: they despised all my reproof.
>
> Therefore shall they eat of the fruit of their own way, and be filled with their own devices. For the turning away of the simple shall slay them, and the prosperity of fools shall destroy them. But whoso hearkeneth unto me shall dwell safely, and shall be quiet from fear of evil" (Proverbs 1:28-33).

Don't wait until it's too late. Start your journey now. Begin to fill in any leadership voids that may exist; partner with someone who can guide you and offer godly counsel. Don't be satisfied with only making sure you are on the road to wisdom. Become a leader. Take someone else with you. This is the journey of a lifetime—destination wisdom!

Points to Ponder

- Are you purposely seeking to develop character in your life?

- Are you fulfilling your destiny?

- Are you modeling godly character for others by doing and teaching? Examine your character and possibly ask a trusted mentor or friend for their analysis as well.

- Are you driving a duct-taped Ford Mustang or a loaded 4Runner?

— Notes —

CHAPTER TWO

1. Bullock, C. Hassell. *An Introduction to the Old Testament Poetic Books*, 1988, Chicago, The Moody Bible Institute, p. 22.

2. *Evangelical Dictionary of Theology*. "Wisdom" K.S. Kantzer, page 1278.

CHAPTER FOUR

1. Barna Group. "The Bible in America: 6 Year Trends" accessed September 28, 2017. https://www.barna.com/research/the-bible-in-america-6-year-trends/

2. Lifeway Research: Americans Are Fond of the Bible, Don't Actually Read It." April 25, 2017 accessed September 28, 2017. http://lifewayresearch.com/2017/04/25/lifeway-research-americans-are-fond-of-the-bible-don't-actually-read-it/

3. *Today in Civil Liberties History*. "President Kennedy Supports Court Ban on Prayer in Schools" accessed September 28, 2017. http://todayinclh.com/?event=president-kennedy-supports-court- ban-on-prayer-in-schools.

CHAPTER FIVE

1. McSpadden, Kevin. "You Now Have a Shorter Attention Span Than a Goldfish" *Time* (magazine) May 14, 2015, http://time.com/3858309/attention-spans-goldfish/ accessed December 16, 2017.

CHAPTER SEVEN

1. Hammerstein II, Oscar. "Do-Re-Mi" - *The Sound of Music,* 1959, Richard Rogers and Oscar Hammerstein II.

2. Barna Group. "Most Twenty-Somethings Put Christianity on the Shelf Following Spiritually Active Teen Years" - https://www.barna.com/research/most-twentysomethings-put-christianity- on-the-shelf-following-spiritually-active-teen-years/

CHAPTER EIGHT

1. Henry, Dana. "Who Causes More Car Accidents? The Data May Surprise You?" *Safety Resource Center.* February 22, 2017. https://www.trafficsafetystore.com/blog/who-causes-accidents/ (accessed November 18, 2017).

CHAPTER NINE

1. McDonough, Patricia. "TV Viewing Among Kids At An Eight Year High." http://www.nielsen.com/us/en/insights/news/2009/tv-viewing-among-0kids-at-an-eight-year-high.html

2. Hamilton, Brady, Martin, Joyce A., and Ventura, Stephanie Jr. National Center for Health Statistics, "National Vital Statistics Report." https://www.cdc.gov/nchs/data/nvsr/nvsr62/nvsr62_03.pdf

3. Campbell, Alexia Fernandez. *The Atlantic,* "Why Are So Many Millennials Having Children Out of Wedlock?" https://www.theatlantic.com/business/archive/2016/07/why-are-so-many-millennials-having-children-out-of-wedlock/491753/

4. Cherlin, Andrew J., Talbert, Elizabeth, and Yasutake, Suzumi. John Hopkins University, "Changing Fertility Regimes and the Transition to Adulthood: Evidence from a Recent Cohort" http://krieger.jhu.edu/sociology/wp-content/uploads/sites/28/2012/02/Read-Online.pdf

5. Yale Global Online. http://yaleglobal.yale.edu/content/out-wedlock-births-rise-worldwide.

6. Barna Group. "Evangelism is Most Effective Among Kids." https://www.barna.com/research/evangelism-is-most-effective-among-kids/

7. "Jesus Loves the Little Children." Words by C. Herbert Woolston, music by George F. Root.

8. Ham, Ken and Beemer, Brit, 2009. *Already Gone: Why Your Kids Will Quit Church and What You Can Do to Stop It*, Master Books, page 106 -107.

9. Gallop. "Religion" - http://www.gallup.com/poll/1690/religion.aspx.

10. Barna Group. "The State of the Church 2016" - https://www.barna.com/research/state- church - 2016/

11. "The Demographic Characteristics of Linguistic and Religious Groups in Switzerland," Warner Haug, Philippe Wanner; *The*

Demographic Characteristics of National Minorities in Certain European States, Volume 2, Werner Haug, Paul Compton, Youssef Courbage (editors). Council of European Publishing, Germany, January 2000, as summarized at: http://www.christianpost.com/news/fathers-key-to-their-childrens-faith-51331/

12. The Pew Research Center. "The Gender Gap in Religion Around the World." http://www.pewforum.org/2016/03/22/the-gender-gap-in-religion-around-the-world/

13. McClendon, David. "Gender gap in religious service attendance has narrowed in U.S." Pew Research Center, http://www.pewresearch.org/fact-tank/2016/05/13/gender-gap-in-religious- service-attendance-has-narrowed-in-u-s/

14. National Association of Evangelicals. "Evangelicals Choose Public Schools." https://www.nae.net/evangelicals-choose-public-schools/

CHAPTER TEN

1. Walker, W.L. *International Standard Bible Encyclopedia.* "Fool; Folly" Blue Letter Bible 2017. https://www.blueletterbible.org/search/Dictionary/viewTopic.cfm?topic=IT0003501#isbeDiv (accessed November 24, 2017).

2. Henry, Matthew, *Matthew Henry's Concise Commentary,* E-sword.

3. Spurgeon, Charles, *Treasury of David,* E-sword.

4. Pew Research Center. "America's Changing Religious Landscape" May 12, 2015. http://www.pewforum.org/2015/05/12/americas-changing-religious-landscape/accessed November 24, 2017.

5. Gervais, Will M., and Maxine B. Najile. "How many atheists are there?" University of Kentucky Psychology, n.d.https://psyarxiv.com/edzda

CHAPTER ELEVEN

1. Dobson, Dr. James. *Brining Up Boys.* Wheaton: Tyndale House Publishers, Inc., 2001, page 232.

2. IBID, page 237.

3. Smith, Brendan L., American Psychology Association. "The Case Against Spanking." http://www.apa.org/monitor/2012/04/spanking. aspx, accessed November 25, 2017.

4. Mclendon, David and Lipka, Michael, Pew Research Center. "Why people with no religion are expected to decline as a share of the world's population" April 7. 2017.http://www.pewresearch.org/ fact-tank/2017/04/07/why-people-with-no-religion-are- projected-to-decline-as-a-share-of-the-worlds-population/, accessed November 25, 2017.

5. Center on the Developing Child. "The Science of Early Childhood Development (InBrief)." Harvard University, 2007. https:// developingchild.harvard.edu/resources/inbrief-science-of-ecd/ (accessed February 10, 2018).

CHAPTER TWELVE

1. Issa, Erin El. "2017 American Household Credit Card Debt Study." Nerd Wallet. September, 2017. https://www.nerdwallet.com/blog/ average-credit-card-debt-household/ (accessed December 12, 2017).

2. Henry, Matthew, *Matthew Henry's Concise Commentary.*

3. Huddleston, Cameron. "More Than Half of Americans Have Less Than $1,000 in Savings in 2017." *GoBankingRates.* September 12, 2017. https://www.gobankingrates.com/saving- money/ half-americans-less-savings-2017/ (accessed December 4, 2017).

CHAPTER THIRTEEN

1. Blake, John, CNN. "Why Young Christians Aren't Waiting Anymore." http://religion.blogs.cnn.com/2011/09/27/ why-young-christians-arent-waiting-anymore/

2. Relevant Magazine. "Religious Dating Sites: More than Half of Users Surveyed Are OK with Premarital Sex." https://relevantmagazine.com/slices/ religious-dating-sites-more-half-users-surveyed-are-ok-premarital-sex.

3. NAE. "Sex and Unexpected Pregnancies: What Evangelical Millennials Think and Practice." https://www.nae.net/ sex-and-unexpected-pregnancies/

4. Grey Matters Research and Consulting, "Evangelical Millennials Say Sex Outside of Marriage Is Wrong, but Behavior Does Not Always Match Beliefs." http://greymatterresearch.com/index_files/millennials_2.htm

5. Luck, Kenny, Charisma News. "Sexual Atheism: Christian Dating Data Reveals a Deeper Spiritual Malaise" - https://www.charismanews.com/opinion/43436-sexual-atheism-christian-dating-data- reveals-a-deeper-spiritual-malaise.

6. Barna Group. "Majority of Americans Now Believe in Cohabitation." https://www.barna.com/research/majority-of-americans-now-believe-in-cohabitation/

7. Barna Group. "Should Sex Ed Teach Abstinence? Most Americans Say Yes." https://www.barna.com/research/sex-ed-teach-waiting-say-yes/?utm_source=Barna+Update+List&utm_campaign=4282c6a738-EMAIL_CAMPAIGN_2017_09_5&utm_medium=email&utm_term=0_8560a0e52e- 4282c6a738-180659861&mc_cid=4282c6a738&mc_eid=dff85f9546.

8. Blair, Leonardo. "Abstinance Author, Pastor Joshua Harris Apologizes for Telling Christians Not to Date in, *I Kissed Dating Goodbye.*" Christian Post http://www.christianpost.com/news/abstinence-author-pastor-joshua-harris-apologizes-for- telling-christians-not-to-date-in-i-kissed-dating-goodbye-168650/

10. Weekend Edition Sunday. NPR, "Former Evangelical Pastor Rethinks His Approach to Courtship." http://www.npr.org/2016/07/10/485432485/former-evangelical-pastor-rethinks-his-approach-to-courtship

Chapter Fourteen

1. Medred, Craig, Anchorage Daily News. "'Blood Knife' Tale Fails to Pass Basic Examination" http://www.wolfsongnews.org/news/Alaska_current_events_2577.html

2. Gladwell, Malcolm. *Blink.* New York City, NY: Little, Brown and Company, Time Warner Book Group, 2005, pages 155-159.

3. Britannica. "Ermine" http://library.eb.com/levels/referencecenter/article/ermine/32924.

4. Butt, Kyle. Apologetics Press. "The Ermine: A Protector of Purity." http://www.apologeticspress.org/DiscoveryPubPage.aspx?pub=2&issue=1211&article=2583.

CHAPTER FIFTEEN

1. Scholastic. "Classroom Behavior Problems Increasing, Teachers Say." https://www.scholastic.com/teachers/articles/teaching-content/classroom-behavior-problems- increasing-teachers-say/, accessed October 31, 2017.

2. Primary Sources: 2012 report available at: http://www.scholastic.com/primarysources/PrimarySources3rdEditionWithAppendix.pdf.

3. Mayo Clinic staff. "Anger Management: 10 tips to tame your temper." Mayo Clinic. https://www.mayoclinic.org/healthy-lifestyle/adult-health/in-depth/anger-management/art- 20045434, accessed October 31, 2017.

4. American Safety Council. "Aggressive Driving and Road Rage." http://www.safemotorist.com/articles/road_rage.aspx, accessed October 31, 2017.

5. Johnson, Tamara. "Nearly 80 Percent of Drivers Express Significant Anger, Aggression or Road Rage" - American Automobile Association (AAA). http://newsroom.aaa.com/2016/07/nearly-80-percent-of-drivers-express-significant-anger- aggression-or-road-rage/ accessed October 31, 2017

6. Segan, Sascha. "Sports Rage Fight Latest in Series" ABC News. http://abcnews.go.com/US/story?id=96558&page=1 accessed October 31, 2017.

7. Doheny, Kathleen. CBS News, "1 in 10 Deaths Among U.S. Tied to Alcohol." https://www.cbsnews.com/news/1-in-10-deaths-among-us-adults-tied-to-alcohol/accessed November 1, 2017.

Bibliography

American Safety Council. "Aggressive Driving and Road Rage." Safe Motorist. n.d. http://www.safemotorist.com/articles/road_rage.aspx (accessed October 31, 2017).

Andrews, Julie. "Do-Re-Mi." *The Sound of Music*. Comp. II Oscar Hammerstein. 1959.

Aquinas, St. Thomas. "Question 47. Prudence, considered in itself." In The Summa Theologiæ of St. Thomas Aquinas by St. Thomas Aquinas. 2016.

Barna Group. "Evangelism Is Most Effective Among Kids." October 11, 2004. https://www.barna.com/research/evangelism-is-most-effective-among-kids/ (accessed August 20, 2017).

—. "Majority of Americans Now Believe in Cohabitation." Barna. June 24, 2016. https://www.barna.com/research/majority-of-americans-now-believe-in-cohabitation/ (accessed October 1, 2017).

—. "Most Twenty-Somethings Put Christianity on the Shelf Following Spiritually Active Teen Years." September 11, 2006. https://www.barna.com/research/most-twentysomethings-put-christianity-on-the-shelf-following-spiritually-active-teen-years/ (accessed September 10, 2017).

—. "Should Sex Ed Teach Abstinence? Most Americans Say Yes." Barna. September 5, 2017. https://www.barna.com/research/sex-ed-teach-waiting-say yes/?utm_source=Barna+Update+List&utm_campaign=4282c6a738-EMAIL_CAMPAIGN_2017_09_5&utm_medium=email&utm_term=0_8560a0e52e-4282c6a738-180659861&mc_cid=4282c6a738&mc_eid=dff85f9546 (accessed October 1, 2017).

—. "The Bible in America: 6 Year Trends." barna.com. June 15, 2016. https://www.barna.com/research/the-bible-in-america-6-year-trends/ (accessed September 28, 2017).

—. "The State of the Church 2016." September 15, 2016. https://www.barna.com/research/state-church-2016/ (accessed August 25, 2017).

Blair, Leonardo. "Abstinence Author, Pastor Joshua Harris, Apologizes for Telling Christians Not to Date in I Kissed Dating Goodbye." *Christian Post.* August 26, 2016. http://www.christianpost.com/news/abstinence-author-pastor-joshua-harris-apologizes-for-telling-christians-not-to-date-in-i-kissed-dating-goodbye-168650/ (accessed July 30, 2017).

Blake, John. "Why Young Christians Aren't Waiting Anymore." CNN. September 27, 2011. http://religion.blogs.cnn.com/2011/09/27/why-young-christians-arent-waiting-anymore/ (accessed September 5, 2017).

Brady E. Hamilton. Ph.D., M.P.H. Joyce A. Martin, and M.A. and Stephanie J. Ventura. Births: Preliminary Data for 2012. Division of Vital Statistics, National Center for Health Statistics, Washington, D.C. Center for Disease Control, 2013.

Britanica. Ermine. n.d. 2017 (accessed September 10, 2017).

Bullock, C. Hassell. *An Introduction to the Old Testament Poetic Books*, Chicago: The Moody Bible Institute, 1988.

Campbell, Alexia Fernandez. "Why Are So Many Millennials Having Children Out of Wedlock?" The Atlantic. July 18, 2016. https://www.theatlantic.com/business/archive/2016/07/why-are-so-many-millennials-having-children-out-of-wedlock/491753/ (accessed August 20, 2017).

Center on the Developing Child. "The Science of Early Childhood Development (InBrief)." Harvard University, 2007.

Chamie, Joseph. Yale Global Online. March 16, 2017. https://yaleglobal.yale.edu/content/out-wedlock-births-rise-worldwide (accessed August 20, 2017).

Cherlin, Andrew J., Elizabeth Talbert and Suzumi Yasutake. "Changing Fertility Regimes and the Transition to Adulthood." Johns Hopkins University, n.d.

Comoreanu, Alina. "2017 Credit Card Debt Study: Trends & Insights." WalletHub. November 9, 2017. https://wallethub.com/edu/credit-card-debt-study/24400/ (accessed December 6, 2017).

Craven, S. Michael. "Fathers: Key to Their Children's Faith." The Christian Post, June 19, 2011. https://www.christianpost.com/news/fathers-key-to-their-childrens-faith-51331/ (accessed August 25, 2017).

Dobson, Dr. James. *Bringing Up Boys*, Wheaton: Tyndale House Publishers, Inc., 2001.

—. *The New Dare to Discipline*, Wheaton: Tyndale House Publishers, Inc., 1992.

Doheny, Kathleen. "1 in 10 Deaths Among U.S. Adults Tied to Alcohol." CBS News. June 26, 2014. https://www.cbsnews.com/news/1-in-10-deaths-among-us-adults-tied-to-alcohol/ (accessed November 1, 2017).

Evangelical Dictionary of Theology. n.d.

Gallop. n.d. http://news.gallup.com/poll/1690/religion.aspx (accessed August 20, 2017).

Gervais, Will M., and Maxine B. Najile. "How Many Atheists Are There?" Psychology, University of Kentucky, n.d.

Gladwell, Malcolm. *Blink*. New York: Little, Brown and Company, 2005.

Grey Matter Research & Consulting. "Evangelical Millennials Say Sex Outside of Marriage Is Wrong." Grey Matter, December 3, 2012. http://greymatterresearch.com/index_files/Millennials_2.htm (accessed October 1, 2017).

Ham, Ken, and Beemer, Brit. *Already Gone: Why Your Kids Will Quit the Church and What You Can Do to Stop It.*, Master Books, 2009.

Harris, Joshua, interview by Rachel Martin. "Former Evangelical Pastor Rethinks His Approach to Courtship." Weekend Edition (July 10, 2016).

Henry, Dana. "Who Causes More Car Accidents? The Data May Surprise You" Safety Resource Center. February 22, 2017. https://www.trafficsafetystore.com/blog/who-causes-accidents/ (accessed November 18, 2017).

Henyr, Matthew. *Matthew Henry's Concise Commentary*. E-Sword, Rick Myers, 2017.

Herbster, Carl & Hurst, Randy. *Against the Tide: Reclaiming Authentic Christian Education*, Greenville: Ambassador International, 2011.

Huddleston, Cameron. "More Than Half of Americans Have Less Than $1,000 in Savings in 2017." GoBankingRates. September 12, 2017. https://www.gobankingrates.com/saving-money/half-americans-less-savings-2017/ (accessed December 4, 2017).

Issa, Erin El. "2017 American Household Credit Card Debt Study." Nerdwallet. September 2017. https://www.nerdwallet.com/blog/average-credit-card-debt-household/ (accessed December 12, 2017).

Johnson, Tamara. "Nearly 80 Percent of Drivers Express Significant Anger, Aggression or Road Rage." AAA News Room. July 14, 2016. http://newsroom.aaa.com/2016/07/nearly-80-percent-of-drivers-express-significant-anger-aggression-or-road-rage/ (accessed October 31, 2017).

Butt, Kyle. "The Ermine: A Protector of Purity." Discover Apologetics Press. 2016. http://www.apologeticspress.org/DiscoveryPubPage. aspx?pub=2&issue=1211&article=2583 (accessed September 15, 2017).

Lifeway Research. "Lifeway Research: Americans Are Fond of the Bible, Don't Actually Read It." lifewayresearch.com. April 25, 2017. http://lifewayresearch.com/2017/04/25/lifeway-research-americans-are-fond-of-the-bible-dont-actually-read-it/ (accessed September 28, 2017).

Lucky, Kenny. "Sexual Atheism: Christian Dating Data Reveals a Deeper Spiritual Malaise." Charisma News. April 9, 2014. https://www.charismanews.com/opinion/43436-sexual-atheism-christian-dating-data-reveals-a-deeper-spiritual-malaise (accessed October 1, 2017).

Mayo Clinic. "Anger Management: 10 Tips to Tame Your Temper." Mayo Clinic. March 4, 2017. https://www.mayoclinic.org/healthy-lifestyle/adult-health/in-depth/anger-management/art-20045434 (accessed October 31, 2017).

McClendon, David. "Gender gap in religious service attendance has narrowed in U.S." Pew Research Center. May 13, 2016. http://www.pewresearch.org/fact-tank/2016/05/13/gender-gap-in-religious-service-attendance-has-narrowed-in-u-s/ (accessed August 27, 2017).

McClendon, David, and Michael Lipka. "Why People with No Religion Are Expected to Decline As a Share of the World's Population." Pew Research Center. April 7, 2017. http://www.pewresearch.org/fact-tank/2017/04/07/why-people-with-no-religion-are-projected-to-decline-as-a-share-of-the-worlds-population/ (accessed November 25, 2017).

McDonough, Patricia. "TV Viewing Among Kids At an Eight Year High." October 26, 2009, http://www.nielsen.com/us/en/insights/news/2009/tv-viewing-among-kids-at-an-eight-year-high.html (accessed August 20, 2017).

McSpadden, Kevin. "You Now Have a Shorter Attention Span Than a Goldfish" *Time* (magazine), May 14, 2015. http://time.com/3858309/attention-spans-goldfish/ (accessed December 16, 2017).

Medred, Craig. "Blood Knife Tale Fails to Pass Basic Examination." Wolf Song News, January 27. 2008. http://www.wolfsongnews.org/news/Alaska_current_events_2577.html (accessed October 1, 2017).

Mishel, Walter. *The Marshmallow Test*, New York, Little, Brown and Company, 2014.

National Association of Evangelicals, "Evangelicals Choose Public Schools" August 2012. https://www.nae.net/evangelicals-choose-public-schools/ (accessed September 1, 2017).

Ortwein, Mary. "Prudence and Wisdom." A Catholic Moment: Daily Mass Readings and Reflections, June 2, 2015. http://www.acatholic.org/prudence-and-wisdom/ (accessed December 7, 2017).

Pew Research Center. "America's Changing Landscape" May 12, 2015. http://www.pewforum.org/2015/05/12/americas-changing-religious-landscape/ (accessed November 24, 2017).

Pew Research. "The Gender Gap in Religion Around the World" March 22, 2016. http://www.pewforum.org/2016/03/22/the-gender-gap-in-religion-around-the-world/ (accessed August 27, 2017).

Relevant. "Religious Dating Sites: More than Half of Users Surveyed Are OK with Premarital Sex." Relevant Magazine. January 27, 2014. https://relevantmagazine.com/slices/religious-dating-sites-more-half-users-surveyed-are-ok-premarital-sex (accessed October 1, 2017).

Scholastic and Bill & Melinda Gates Foundation. "Primary Sources: A project of Scholastic and the Bill & Melinda Gates Foundation" 2012.

Scholastic. "Classroom Behavior Problems Increasing, Teachers Say" Scholastic. n.d. https://www.scholastic.com/teachers/articles/teaching-content/classroom-behavior-problems-increasing-teachers-say/ (accessed October 31, 2017).

Segan, Sascha I. "Sports Rage Fight Latest in Series" ABC News. July 11, 2017. http://abcnews.go.com/US/story?id=96558&page=1 (accessed October 31, 2017).

Smith, Brendan L. "The Case Against Spanking" Monitor on Psychology (American Psychology Association) 43, no. 4 (April 2012).

Spurgeon, Charles H., *Treasury of David*. 11.1.0. Vols. E-Sword. Rick Myers, 2017.

Sri, Edward. "The Art of Living: The First Step of Prudence" Lay Witness, May/June 2009.

Strong, James. *Strong's Concordance* n.d.

Today in Civil Liberties History. "President Kennedy Supports Court Ban on Prayer in Schools" n.d. http://todayinclh.com/?event=president-kennedy-supports-court-ban-on-prayer-in-schools (accessed September 28, 2017).

Walker, W.L. *International Standard Bible Encyclopedia*, "Fool; Folly." Blue Letter Bible. 2017. https://www.blueletterbible.org/search/Dictionary/viewTopic.cfm?topic=IT0003501#isbeDiv (accessed November 24, 2017).

Werner Haug, Paul Compton, Youssef Courbage. "The Demographic Characteristics of Linguistic and Religious Groups in Switzerland." The demographic of national minorities in certain European states, Volume 2, January 2000.

Made in the USA
Middletown, DE
14 February 2020